Date Your Clients

Date Your Clients

Authored by

KAILASH C PINJANI

Disclaimer

SUPER FAST AUTHOR
www.superfastauthor.com

Registered Office- 604, Mayur Vatika, Dapodi Pune 411001
Website: https://www.superfastauthor.com
Email: superfastauthor@gmail.com

First Published by SUPERFASTAUTHOR 2020

Title: DATE YOUR CLIENTS

LIMITS OF LIABILITY/DISCLAIMER OF WARRANTY

Index

Dedication

I dedicate this book to lovers, sales guys, and entrepreneurs. I wish them lot of success & power to achieve everything they dream.

Acknowledgement to My Dream Team

I have lot of gratitude for my team; this book, rather this life would not be fulfilled and complete without them.

Thank you, God, for being part of my team and always sending signals that I am blessed. Thank you for implanting dreams and giving me a purpose in my life. Thank you for making me a channel of your wisdom. Always making sure that the right people, especially my mentors, cross my path to help me learn and placing me at the right place at the right time. Thank you for putting me through life learnings and making me achieve my dreams.

Thank you, my family, for being part of my team, making me stronger and helping me focus on my life's purpose.

Preface

Sales, a scary word for lots of people but it is a skill most essential to have a happy life. Yes, happy life.

You may be thinking that sales is essential skill only for sales guys and I am a *housewife or a student or operations manager or software engineer* or whatever, what is in it for me. Well to tell you that it is a wake-up call for you today.

If you are holding this book then it is no coincidence. One thing is 100% sure that you are looking to improve your life or profession to higher levels.

This book will surely help those who wants to make their career in sales, but the concepts of this book are valid for everyone who breathes and wants to have a successful life.

Selling, in other words, is persuasion or influencing.

After reading this book, you will never be the same person again.

Every minute we make decisions, we are selling the concept to ourselves for the things we decide to do or not to do. We humans are social animal and deal with lots of people on day to day basis. When we put forward our ideas, thoughts across to them, we are selling. Things will always be in your favour if you are good at selling.

In our less than perfect world having the best skills or being the best person is not good enough. Others should know that too.

THE BEST-KNOWN ALWAYS BEATS THE BEST!

Do you know a person around who knows how to show his best to the world and they keep growing faster in life?

Some people are *biologically* good at marketing themselves; some have challenges with this skill, but it is a learnable skill, and anyone can learn this if you have a deep desire to get success in life.

With the grace of God, I have been *biologically* good at marketing myself.

I was born and brought up in a small city, went to a typical government school, financially deprived family. As a refugee family moved the base in 1947 partition, money was a challenge in our house. Though my parents worked extremely hard to make sure that gave me a better life than they had.

These hardships have made me a better person, but I believe the most important one is I knew how to market myself well. That got me the highest possible places in life, and this keeps happening.

I always wanted to teach the skill of marketing to friends, family and people around me, but the word sales alone scared them away.

But one beautiful morning I realized that the creator of this body has given us some basic burning needs in our body and those needs pushes us to keep improving.

Two most essential needs burning inside us are Hunger and Love.

From ancient times hunger drives us to work hard to look for food. Though the definition of hunger has changed with time with mere food to better house, car, holidays, or materialistic achievements.

Love, the emotion of love brings into being in a state of mind. Because of ignorance on this subject, we avoid talking about it. Most people connect love with physical alignment, so with this improper influence, people are biased about it.

Love is one of the most powerful needs of humans. When driven by this need, we develop the best of imagination, persistence, courage, will power, creative ability that is unknown to us.

This need is so strong that MAN since ages, for love runs the risk of life and reputation. If this deep fire is harnessed and redirected along the line, it can help us develop imagination, persistence, courage, will power and creative ability.

When we all touch puberty, the hormones in our body start playing and teaching us the game of Love & Relationship. We start indulging in impressing opposite gender or **naturally learn the art of dating**.

The successful principles of dating inspire the principles of sales in this book. I feel the process of successful dating, and successful sales are the same.

Read it, connect to your life, have fun, and get these principles you already know from dating and align them to your life or your profession.

I am a proud and Successful Sales Guy....

Kailash C Pinjani

Word from Author

"Intent gives Superpower to Content."

I have written this book from my personal experiences and have no desire to put anyone down or give wrong advice to anyone. Concepts written in the book are typical sales process and have given me my results. I have tried my best not to be biased while writing, as well as providing the best possible way to achieve results.

Men are from Mars, and Women are from Venus. I am a Man, who think and act like a man. In my book, I have given dating examples from my perspectives, and any woman reading this book may find flaws. I would love to get feedback to improve my perspective about looking towards relationships.

All principles in my book are related to long term relations with a woman or with clients. These principles will not work for a fling, one-night stands, for post-marital affairs, get rich quick schemes, and non-value driven salespeople or companies.

It is my humble request to keep your old learnings aside while reading this book and give my concepts a chance to be evaluated. Try these concepts in your life and career for a minimum of 90 days to see the magic. If you do not like these concepts, you are free to throw back these concepts to the universe for others to get success.

Feel free to connect to me on kailashcpinjani@gmail.com for your feedback and share how concepts in the book changed your life.

CHAPTER
One

Who Wants to Learn Sales

"You miss 100% of the shots you don't take."
–Wayne Gretzky

We all are in the game of selling every minute of our life from birth to death.....

How many of you think you don't need to learn the skill of selling, let me tell you that you are wrong.

Let me tell you quick scenarios...

Two friends on free weekend decide to go for a movie. One is a fan of Salman khan, and other is a fan of Sharukh khan. There is an argument, which movie to go or. Both want to go for their choice and want to go together.

Which movie will they see? It will depend on who has better selling skill.

When you are teaching young children to study hard to get good marks in school, how well a child will study will depend on how well parents or school teachers can sell the concept of studies to the kid.

A mother convinces her kid to eat Louki Sabji which the kid doesn't like. In this case, the mother is selling louki and good health to the kid.

When you are sitting in a job interview, for the same job, many people are also applying. Will you get that job over many others, will depend on how excellent skills you have selling yourself?

As an HR of the company when you finalize a candidate, the chances of his joining your organization depends on how excellent selling skill HR has, as the same candidate is considering at the same time many other companies to join.

When in college and you like a girl or a boy, the chances that you will have them as your girlfriend or boyfriend will also depend on how good you are at selling yourself.

Every minute we have to decide on something, and if in that decision others are involved then you are in a situation of selling. Things will always be in your favour if you are good at selling.

The art of selling says that you can't be pushy. People should consider your ideas and suggestions naturally without any force.

It has a lot to do with psychology because do you remember a situation where you don't want to buy something or do something, but you lost control over yourself and did that or bought that. Why? Because the other person is playing psychologically with you and you consider his buying proposal.

Selling, in other words, is persuasion or influencing.

Everyone every day we sell knowingly or unknowingly.

The big question is whether intentionally you want to learn the skill and sell better, or you will keep saying that I am not lucky enough.

You may think you have done good in life till now without selling much so why learn now. Let me tell you the world is becoming far more competitive as we live in the digital era. The kind of tools and technologies we have changed the way we interacted. We have become global.

Earlier when you were chasing a girl of your dreams in your gali or neighbourhood, you were only competing with other boys of your gali, mohalla or maximum your city.

Now in the digital era, your world is in your mobile (Facebook, Instagram, Whatsapp, and not to forget Tinder) and now to get the same girl you are competing with the world. She has better choices and options.

Similarly now your customers can google, Justdial, Indiamart or many such websites and find many other vendors to sell and supply the things you sell and supply.

The competition has increased as digital innovations have broken the boundaries of geography.

***The world is changing, and the question is,
are you changing!!!***

CHAPTER Two

You are the Product

***Can you LOVE someone else,
even if you don't LOVE yourself?***

The first rule to dating is (and even for Life); what you think about yourself is more important than what the other girl or your clients think about you.

If you don't think good about yourself, then there is not even a tiny chance that the girl you are dreaming will feel good about you.

The first rule is to be yourself, don't pretend to be someone who you are not. As truth will prevail itself soon and then it will be a problematic heartbreaking situation.

The second rule is that everyone may not quite like you if you are yourself, but that is **OK**. As in the end, the perfect fit will find you and will love you the way you are.

How to love yourself is very simple yet very difficult as you spend most of our time with yourself unintentionally. There are few rules to love yourself....

- Observer yourself so you know how you behave
- Understand why you behave in specific ways
- Accept yourself the way you are
- Don't pretend to be someone who you are not
- If you think some behaviour is to be improved, please do
- Have fun with yourself
- Remove negative beliefs about yourself

- Avoid Perfectionism
- Believe in small improvements
- Have positive affirmations

You should have the right image about yourself and *accept your flaws*. Work on flaws to reduce, yes reduce not eliminate because elimination takes time. We always self-sabotage our self and think I am not pleasant; I am not handsome; I am no good. This self-sabotaging is the biggest hurdle in your life. Lots of people try to mask these flaws and start looking fabricated and unreal. The key is accepting, improve and move. Once you know yourself start projecting right image of yourself to the prospective partner. She will start showing interest in you.

Give her time to accept you the way you are, don't hurry in relation. She will time test you, and with time the relationship will improve. That's right, what comes quickly, goes quick.

You may not get some matches done, but that is fine as you are looking for a perfect match if it finds you it will last long. On a lighter note, enjoy and learn from the wrong ones till you find the right one.

Anything that you want to sell has to be sold to yourself first.

In the situation of selling when you go and meet prospective customers.

The same is true for people as well;
they buy you first as a person,

then your product and service and

then the company where you work.

You cannot sell your product or service if you don't feel good about yourself in selling it or if you don't feel that your product or service adds value to your customer life.

You can't sell a product and service until you have bought the product yourself first. Because when you buy you believe that it has value and there are people like you who will buy it.

Many insurance companies make their own agents or employees buy their products first so as to increase their belief and faith in the product. Then only they will convince their clients with 100% enthusiasm.

In my profession, I work with many business coaches who sell high ticket services to their clients. One of my clients who works as a business coach is struggling to sell mentoring and coaching to his clients for INR 12 Lakh a year. When we were discussing the probable reason, it came out that deep down, he has never paid similar amount for similar services to other coaches.

How can you sell something which you will never buy?

Especially in high ticket sales, your prospective customer needs to like you, so he is biased towards you. Let me explain this concept psychologically.

People don't think how they feel,

They don't say how they think, &

They don't do what they say.

People always do what they feel.

Whether dating or sales, someone who is a stranger to you today, may become your date or customer tomorrow. So, let's understand the strange behavior of strangers.

When you meet your prospective buyers and explain to them about your product/services, as they are listening to you the first time, they will have few psychological fears or risks in mind. They may not be aware of this as this happens very deep down.

What could be those quantifiable risks....

1. Risk of Time

2. Risk of Money

3. Risk of Emotions (Cannot be measured)

We live our lives at our center, and we create a virtual circle around us. This circle is like a fence, people inside this fence will be known and trusted people, and outside of this fence will be unknown or strangers.

When you meet someone for the first time as a stranger, you are outside of their circle of trust.

Now the big question is how you can get inside the circle of trust to make the long-lasting win-win relationships quickly.

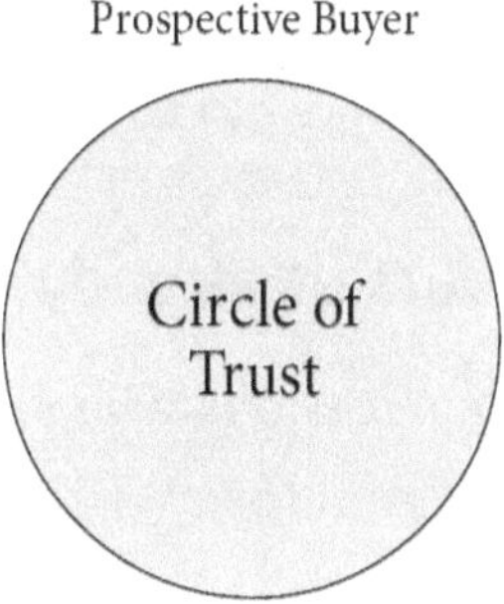

The answer is straightforward:

- Reduce the risk of time to minimal

- Reduce the risk of money to as low as possible

- Reduce the risk of emotional loss to a minimum

As risks go down to minimal, it becomes easy for other people to start a relationship with you. And slowly you start progressing towards circle of trust. The deeper inside you go, you will be highly trusted.

There are other rules as well to become fantastic and highly trusted personality, so market starts liking you:-

- Be true to what you say

- Have the highest possible integrity inside you

- Wear a smile as frequently as you are breathing

- Keep high standards

- Be grounded

- Always believe in the value you are bringing on the table.

Being a good salesperson starts from being a fantastic person internally and ethically. Everyone has positives and negatives characteristics but learn to focus on your positives. Let's answer a few questions to know yourself:

Do you market yourself already??

Can you think of five occasions when you have marketed yourself in the last few months? Write them down here:

1. ....

2. ....

3. ....

4. ....

5. ....

Why did you have to market yourself on these occasions? Write them down:

1. ....

2. ....

3. ....

4. ....

5. ....

How exactly you marketed yourself?

1. ....

2. ....

3. ....

4. ....

5. ....

Think of five occasions when you lost out because you didn't present yourself in the best light through inadequate self-marketing:

The problems of self-marketing:

There is a significant potential problem in self-marketing, people may find you pushy and outspoken. This may not always be damaging especially if your intentions are very pure to bring value to the relationship.

Another way to handle the situation is to give people space after you have done your job showing them real 10X value. Space allows people to think with a calm mind and unbiased thinking process. I call it biased for your mindset as Newton's Third Law of Motion says that to every action, there is an equal and opposite reaction. Giving space after your sales, encourages and pull back clients to you.

Though there could be some challenges with self-marketing but not doing will attract more enormous problems in your life.

In the end, you don't win all the clients, and it is essential too as you only allow the right clients to come to your life. Every client is not yours; One wrong client can get you in the wrong mental state and push your energies down.

Knowing yourself better:

I have designed many questions in this chapter to know yourself better. This is going to be hard for you, as you may not answer many questions, but that is OK.

These questions will help you know yourself better instead of doing market research on yourself. This isn't the psychology test but a quick way to understand yourself.

This test not only tells you what kind of person you are but also may give you some area to improve. I recommend you to do this test multiple times as we keep changing, improving and growing.

This test is divided into multiple sections for better understanding.

Rate yourself on a scale of 10 for each question.

How organised are you?

Are you able to get things done as required?

Do you do things when it is to be done, or you wait
till the last minute?

Are you punctual and follow your time commitment

given to others? ☐

Are you able to complete your office / school / college projects on time? ☐

Do you plan things ahead of time? ☐

Do you organize systems or processes for doing things for yourself or others? ☐

Do you plan your day? ☐

Do you make a list of things to be done? ☐

Do you write the shopping list? ☐

When you are going on holiday, do you make a list of things to be taken or places to visit? ☐

Do you buy other's birthday gift/presents in advance? ☐

Do you finish festival shopping in advance to save yourself from rush? ☐

Are you the one who organizes parties and events for family and friends? ☐

How motivated are you?

If you need to acquire a new hobby or skill, do you go out and do it? ☐

How successful are you acquiring new skills? ☐

Do you generally have the energy to do the things you want to do? ☐

Do you spend much time on social media or TV? ☐

Do you have stamina or energy to carry the day? ☐

Do you take time to play sports / go to the gym regularly? ☐

Do you find it easy to do things on your own? ☐

Do you work on your own? ☐

Do you always like to have people around you? ☐

When you start doing things, can you continue doing
it without distractions as well? ☐

You are in the middle of an urgent job, and friends drop
by, will you tell him to come after some time? ☐

Do you instead watch TV or Mobile than finishing
the job you don't like to do? ☐

Have you worked longer than required to help someone? ☐

Do you think you are lazy? ☐

Do you think you are hardworking? ☐

When you start something, do you make sure
to finish the task or leave it in between? ☐

Do you play any endurance sports like running
marathons, cross country or triathlon? ☐

Are you a risk-taker?

Are you able to take risks? ☐

Do you try new sports, activities, food or restaurants? ☐

How well do you communicate?

Do people say you talk well? ☐

If someone asks you to explain the plot of a movie scene
that you saw last night, would you do it quickly? ☐

Are you able to persuade others to do things as you want? ☐

Are you able to give good reasons to people to get
things done the way you want? ☐

You understand something, but someone else
does not, can you help him understand the same
in an exciting way? ☐

How well do you get on with others?

Do you think that you get on well with other people? ☐

Can you guide and supervise others so they can do
a good job? ☐

Have you ever sold anything to anyone? ☐

Do you always want to go out and meet people? ☐

How decisive are you?

Are you good at making decisions? ☐

Do friends come to you for advice on their decisions? ☐

Do you make decisions very often? ☐

Do you postpone making big decisions? ☐

Do you make generally right decisions? ☐

Are you willing to learn?

Would you make an effort to learn new things? ☐

Would you quickly invest in learning new things? ☐

How easy is it for you to find out the information you need? ☐

How often do you read books? ☐

Are you a planner?

Do you plan things ahead? ☐

Are you able to gaze at potential problems in advance? ☐

How adaptable are you?

Are you a multitasking person? ☐

How flexible are you to things and situations? ☐

How creative are you?

Do you think you're creative? ☐

Do others say you have a good imagination? ☐

Do you love solving crosswords and puzzles? ☐

Do you watch quizzes on TV / Mobile? ☐

Do you come up with new ideas quickly? ☐

What creative thing you do? .... ☐

How do you handle the pressure?

How well do you cope up with pressure? ☐

Do you try to shy away from problems or
situations generally? ☐

How do you rate yourself in fighting problems? ☐

If others are in problem, do you help them
in their problem ☐

Action Items

Now I want you to close your eyes and think of 10 people with whom you want to spend time.

1. ....

2. ....

3. ....

4. ....

5. ....

6. ....

7. ....

8. ....

9. ....

10. ....

We like and feel comfortable with people who are like us. Understand what above people like, how they dress, behave or act?

What best describes you? Please circle the words you resemble.

Energetic	Youthful	Old-fashioned	Creative
Capable	Efficient	Powerful	Disciplined
Reliable	Hardworking	Clever	Attractive
Professional	Ambitious	Mature	Co-operative
Assertive	Intelligent	Thoughtful	Intuitive
Friendly	Communicative	Cynical	Adaptable
Understanding	Forthright	Wishy-washy	Principled

Other ....

I hope you know yourself better. Whether you want to be successful in Intimate relationship or sales and marketing, you got to know yourself better and keep improving yourself. If you are a person of great character and grit, no girl or customer can say no to you for anything you ask

Be a Charismatic person and become a magnet.

CHAPTER
Three

The Art of Farming

In the long term, farming will win over hunting.
Are you a hunter or a farmer?

Many people mistake building new relationships as hunting instead of farming.

Have you heard the phrase love at first sight?

I believe love cannot happen at first sight, so the sale. The best way to cultivate relationships and high sales is farming.

Let's look at farmers, how they work?

Do they expect the crop or fruits immediately after seeding?

Have you seen farmers getting demotivated or frustrated that seeds are growing very slow? Even though plants don't give fruits, farmer still patiently water the plants and take care of it. Farmers know that crops will take their own time, so they plan various crops as per their requirement.

Same is true in relations as well as sales. You need to seed the relationship and keep watering, fertilizing and taking care of it, so it gives fruits soon.

Let us look at relationships, once you decide the girl of your dreams, you will have to keep working on growing that relationship. Fruits of relation can come faster than expected too. Human emotions are far more complex than plant growth.

Girl will test you before committing to a serious relationship, also to make sure that you are the right one for her.

There are two types of expectation from girls: -

One is a motherly expectation, where she will behave like your mother. She will expect great things from you, want you to put in your best and grow a lot. She does that because she sees great potential in you and wants you to achieve a lot.

If you don't live up to your potential as per her expectation, you will see lots of troubles in your relation, and it may also end on a wrong note.

Second type of expectation emerges from insecurities. In some cases, the fear and instabilities of the past experience come in the relationship. This may turn in to a challenging relationship. Where you always keep justifying your actions to her.

It would be best if you make sure that the insecurities of other partner are taken care well. Once the trust increases, the relationship goes to a smooth state.

Let's talk about the Business to Business sales now, especially high-ticket sales that depends purely on farming. In B2B sales, many people will test you before you win a deal.

Let me explain various types of roles in the organization

with we have to interact. It is like having relations with multiple partners and trying to make all happy in the sync.

The top 4 roles a sales person usually interacts with: -

1. Gatekeeper
2. Influencer
3. Technical Buyer
4. Decision Maker

1. **Gatekeeper**: This person in the organization will check you and your services and products, and if he likes your product and services, he will take you inside the organization to the right people. You cannot avoid the gatekeeper as he will be easy to access and will generally have a high ego. You got to impress him with your personality more than product and service.

2. **Influencer**: Gatekeeper will take you to the influencer in the organization. Influencers cannot make decisions on your product and service, but in the final decision, his weightage will be highest. Decision-makers cannot entirely go against decisions given by influencer.

3. **Technical Buyer**: This buyer will evaluate the product and service from one of the technical angles only. Those angles could be financial, technology, compliances, or quality assurance. His say in the deal is significant, but it is limited to his technical expertise.

4. **Decision Maker:** This person will make the final decision and nail the deal for you. This person requires lots of information from the gatekeeper, influencer

and technical buyer to nail the deal. He needs an accountable person inside his organization to hand over the accountability post-decision.

The most important thing is that you need to discover an internal champion in your prospective organization. This internal champion will help you sell your products and services. This person can give you some internal information for you to decide your organization specific strategy. This internal champion will have his reason to support you, but the most important is that he has to like you as a person. Once you are in his circle of trust, he will communicate every important thing about the deal. You will have to strengthen your internal champion with enough tools and ready information to help you sell internally. The good scenario is that you influence the internal champion first.

Whether in relation or sales, learn to handle the ego of other parties well. Never allow your ego to become a hindrance. Learn to control others person's ego in your favour.

There are two ways to approach the B2B sales scenario.

1. Top-Down Approach

2. Bottom-up Approach

In the top-down approach, your first point of contact is always the most senior person in the buying cycle, or you can call it a decision-maker. The decision-maker will also tell you to get in touch with other departments during the sales process. Still, the top-down approach process always moves faster. But sales get killed some time during the first few interactions only by the decision-maker. Well that's mostly an advantage and not disadvantage as you save lots of time.

In the bottom-up approach, you start with the gatekeeper and reach the decision-maker who is at the top in the organizational hierarchy.

When farming, you will have to start your farming from the gatekeeper till you reach the decision-maker. One important thing to remember is never to make people feel that you used them, which means when you pass gatekeeper to the influencer to decision-maker, never leave gatekeeper untouched or uninformed.

If officially not possible to inform, then unofficially keep giving him updates of the progress. Keeping everyone in the loop is especially important because your internal champion can turn hostile at any point of time and then you will have to find the next champion.

CHAPTER
Four

*The Game is ON
(Slow-down to speed-up)*

"*Slow down and everything you are chasing will come around.*"

This seems to be a little confusing. How can you slow down to speed-up?

This is about making a decision and optimizing on control over rush. When you are rushing things, you tend to miss lots of important clues that guide you to move in the right direction. One significant turn missed can take you far from the destination.

When you slow down, you tend to get more control over the situation; focus not only on your speed but gather the signs on the way that may be required for course direction and correction. Sometimes high speed, makes you desperate. Desperation kills the enthusiasm in relationships as people might shove away from you.

The best way to avoid desperation is to don't talk or act desperate.

Having desperation and looking like a desperate a** hole are two very different things.

Learn to harness the desperation inside you. People have radar for desperation, and once they smell that you are desperate, they will run away from you.

There are a few signs to access that you are acting like desperate being:

1. Chasing anything that moves.
2. Excessive frequency of calling.
3. Begging for the sale/meeting.
4. Talking way too much than listening
5. Lack discipline
6. Being "too" available.
7. Mind-boggling flexibility.
8. Not following thoroughly.
9. Can't take no for an answer.
10. Rushing the process.

This is very true in dating as well as high ticket sales.

Relationships occurs in a multi-control environment, and minimum of two people are driving this together, so it is essential that their frequency matches up.

You need to love the process you are going through. Every process, dream and destination have the pains to go through. Decide your goals, find out what pains you will have to go through to achieve those goals. Once you are at peace with the pain, the process becomes effortless to follow. Once you start focusing on enjoying the process, you will automatically cut the crap out of life and only follow things you love to follow.

In a relationship, the girl you are following will like to take things slow. As she wants to see how you react to ups and downs, mood swings and are you ready to accept the way she is.

Going slow does not mean being boring; you gotta keep things interesting.

- Keep flirting on
- Hold her hands whenever possible, touch has immense power
- High sense of humour
- Find Creative way to stay connected
- Have your own space and give her too

The sales process is no different in this case; in high-value sales, you will have to take the case but not to look desperate.

Why go slow at specific points of the sales process?

A slower sales pace can cause the customer to put a higher value on your product/service. It's then positioned not as a cheap thrill or a flash in the pan, but as a reliable long-term solution.

Slowing down keeps buyers from becoming overwhelmed and checking out of the sale. Sales guys need to be sensitive to the fact that the selling process may seem simple from their side of the deal. Still, it's undoubtedly more complicated for the buyer. Sales guys do this kind of thing every day; the buyer probably doesn't.

Spending time on providing excellent customer

experience generates more loyal customers. This, in turn, improves customer satisfaction and retention rates, both good indicators for increased referrals, profit, and repeat buys.

Sales guys still need to be productive, proactive, and efficient, but none of these mean 'go as fast as you humanly can.' Knowing when and where to take more time during the sales process is essential.

Especially when creating the relationship, this can be one of the most tempting stages to rush. Still, it's just too important to slow down. Here, the sales guy is laying the foundation for the deal by exploring the buyer's goals, needs, challenges, and wants; all essential information for closing.

When establishing a long-term relationship, building trust between the client and the sales guy takes time. There aren't any shortcuts. And the more complex and more significant the deal, the more time will be required.

Relationship-building requires lots of questions and active listening on the sales guy's part. No adding new information or talking over, just reiterating back what the client said to show acknowledgement and understanding.

Building relationships and trust aren't confined to one particular part of the sales process. Taking time to check back in and make sure the buyer's ideal outcomes or requirements haven't changed allows the sales guy to respond as the deal progresses.

Setting expectations for the sales process is key. Sales guys need to know what a successful deal will look like to work toward it.

Always Under Commit and Over Deliver

Don't commit everything under the sun, which may or may not be required by your customer. Let some things come as bonuses, and that creates long term relations.

The clients will say this company always gives more than they commit, and the sales representative should say I still commit less than my company can deliver.

Key questions sales guys need to know the answers to:

- What are the ideal outcomes?
- What does the timeline look like?
- What actions can help secure these outcomes?
- What happens if a deal is not completed?
- Does the buyer need a solution at a particular time?
- Manage expectations for follow-up and response time.
- The sales guy then knows whether to speed up or maintain their pace based on the buyer's requirements and timing.

Sales guys should confirm with their leads the best way to communicate with them and when to communicate. They should also establish the usual turnaround time for a response, from them and the buyer.

This helps ensure the process will fit within the timelines and keep the sales guy from becoming a nuisance. For example, the guy won't need to follow up multiple times a day if they know that it generally takes two full days for the lead to respond.

The customer buying process may be very complicated. As discussed in earlier chapters, many key stakeholders in the organization take collective decisions on buying decisions.

Let me talk here in Government order, for example…

If you are meeting with the government for a large order, because of the processes involved, the process is generally slow. You got to respect that and try to match up with the speed of government. Don't try to rush things because in the end you will be disappointed.

Building relations with key stakeholders become a vital process as the responsible person will have to prepare the document for inviting bids from interested parties.

If you can create a good relationship your inputs would be part of the bid documents, that's where you already set yourself in a winning situation.

Let me share the secret of winning the government orders, don't share with others.

If you are part of the bid writing process, you win the order. When a bid document is written, the government sets the eligibility criteria's and expectation for companies to bid.

For the government, it is difficult to understand the product or service they need, compared to you as you are an expert in your field. If you are rightly placed inside the sales process and have good rapport with internal champion, government will look at you for guidance for right product / service selection.

When you are giving your input bid process, you need to make sure below:

- **Eliminators** - These points will cut lots of competition, like five years of P&L submission, so you cut all new and small companies. Add enough eliminators to cut most of the competition. You got to know your competitors' strengths and weaknesses.

- **Selectors** - These points are *your strengths* and unique differentiator factors that may not exist with the competition.

Putting right eliminators and selectors will make you win the order by 95% sure. I have won many deals using these simple techniques in large government orders.

The key is going slow and building strong personal relationships with the internal champion.

CHAPTER
Five

You are not competing with anyone

"A horse never runs so fast as when he has other horses to catch up and outpace."

We are not competing with anyone in a race. Still, we need other contenders in life for it to become exciting. Winning becomes more fulfilling when you win against others in the race.

What is the fun in running the race alone and winning?

But infact you are your biggest competition. Other contenders help you to improve.

I have always taken initiatives to speak to all of my important competitors and to be precise, during the course of time some of these competitors have become my good friends now.

In the situation of dating, the girl you are liking will have many other options to go for.

My recommendation is to be yourself and not worry too much about who else is in the race with you. I always advised men, treat your girl like a queen, if you will not do that someone else will treat her like a queen and you may lose your queen. It is equally valid even if you are married.

Treating women like a queen cannot be a selective habit for a man. The man who treats women like a queen will always do that to any girl because he respects girls. Only then he becomes the women charmer, and he has control over what he wants in his life. This is very powerful, and with great power comes great responsibility.

Same is true for sales....

Treat your customers like a king, if you don't do that someone else will treat your customer like a king and you lose the customer.

Make sure to make your **"Customer a King"** :

- Be proactive, not pushy
- Quick response to every query
- Bring 10X value in the deal
- Keep evaluating, how can you give more value
- Appreciate, a Genuine appreciation wherever possible
- Show Trust, give them 100% reliability on you
- Win-Win deal
- Alert and active Customer support
- Proactive Customer Feedback
- Be Approachable
- Listen, Listen & Listen

Let's introspect more.

When you are in the selling situation, how to handle the competition?

Do you think competition can only be won by lowering your PRICE?

Who is your *exact competition*?

Many people and organizations get confused by who their exact competition is.

Your exact competition is the name that would be written on the cheque and purchase order if you lose an order. That order is given to your competition.

There is nothing more frightful than ignorance of your competition.

My rules to handle competition are:

- If competition is weak make them your associate
- If competition is strong, collaborate.
- Always Respect your competition.

How to handle the competition with care:

- Know your competition better
- Know its strengths
- Know its weaknesses
- Know its management
- Know its essential people and their psychic
- Know its customers
- Know its best and worst customers
- Know its failures
- Know its pricing strategy

How will you get the best of information about your competition?

We all have customers, good customers and bad customers. We all have very good customers who are like friends to us. Those few customers or clients can tell us a lot about your competition.

You should evaluate yourself with your top 5 competitors every three months maximum. What new they are doing? What new technologies they have implemented? What new offerings have they devised? Etc.

The evaluation time and process depend on the kind of business which you are in. For some businesses, you should evaluate your competition every day.

Let me share the quick story here:

One of my clients is into high ticket software selling. We were creating the prerequisite for a multi-crore deal in one of the huge government departments.

We played our part well as relations were created very well.

We identified our decision-maker, Influencers, Technical Buyers as well we were able to create and strengthen our internal champion in the deal.

We created a significant part of the bid document; we placed our selector and eliminators in a way that out of 16 organizations quoted, 14 were disqualified on various parameters in bid documents.

Last two selected parties left were us and one of our very strong competition.

We knew precisely everything about our competitor. Their Strengths, Weaknesses, Successful projects, Failed projects, their exact pricing strategy, their past and present history of the management team.

So, if you know so much in detail about your competition, just envision what will be the outcome of the multi corer order deal.

Yes right, Hola, we won the game as per our terms and pricing!!!

CHAPTER
Six

*Choosing the right
game to play*

*"Life is not a game. Still, in this life, we choose the games
we love to play. Just don't waste your energies
on the wrong game "*
- J. R. Rim

The essence of success is in playing the right game, as every win doesn't make you successful. Successful sales strategy is to keep searching for the game you want to play, not to play every game you find. We all have limited time, money & other resources. When you define your goal, be judgmental about whether it is worth chasing or not.

Once the game is on, there is no looking back. So, take time to evaluate thoroughly but never take hasty decisions to jump on playing. Don't keep chasing everything that moves.

Did you ever go out of your way to convince a girl of your assets and qualities?

Take a date for example: from the other side of her table, she looks at you, with a mixture of friendliness and waning interest as you tell her all about your possessions, your solid character and your job.

What you are doing here is called qualification: you're trying to qualify yourself to her. This is the very process what most men don't know.

If it happens the other way round, it can be a major attraction for a woman. Once she has to work for your approval, she'll get quite excited about you. So, how do you get to a point where you are qualifying a girl?

Define your standards

What does "qualification" even mean? If a person is "qualified" for something, they have the traits or skills it takes to live up to a certain standard. That's what you're conveying to a girl when you're telling her about all your accomplishments. You're subtly saying: "This is why I'm good for you". I'm sure you've spent much time figuring out what women generally want in a man (social success, stability, humour, good looks, wealth, charisma...), but can I get an honest answer from you?

When it comes to women, how *much time have you spent defining your standards?*

If you're like me, that idea probably never occurred to you (it only dawned on me when I started to study relationships seriously): now, I'd like you to sit down and define exactly what you want in a woman. Make a list of traits, and keep refining it as you go through your day and watch women, and interact with them.

Only when you have such a clear idea of what you want that you can "screen" a woman accordingly.

Women are already very good at this. They make guys qualify themselves. So now that you have a clear idea of what you want in a woman.

Do you feel any different, as now not only girl is qualifying you, but you also have qualifying criteria's?

If you spent your life trying to kiss hot chicks so you could get a piece of them, I think that this little activity of making this list alone will have changed how you perceive yourself.

What's new? Now, you're the guy who selects women, not the guy who tries to get selected.

Do you know why qualification is essential?

It is because of investment! Not Money only stupid....

There are three types of investment happens in relationship.

1. **Your emotional investment >>> Her emotional Investment**

   This situation, we all have gone through in our college days when you kept thinking a lot about a girl and made lots of plans with her. Maybe she might have not even thought about you. This very imbalance situation and is terrible as this imbalance will drain a lot of your energy out of you and you might not feel good about yourself. This may lead to depression.

2. **Your emotional investment <<< Her emotional Investment**

   This situation is also bad as this will look like you are in a very very possessive relationship. Which builds fear and insecurities, and you will feel very suffocative in this relationship. You would love to run away from this relation, but somethings are holding you.

3. **Your emotional investment = Her emotional Investment.**

   This is the best situation in the relationship. This is not a static situation which once achieved will remain like this always. This is very dynamic in nature, and the imbalances will keep coming.

   Since now you know this, learn to push back to the balancing equation. It's like learning to drive, where initially it's very difficult to do so as your vehicle keep going right or left but yes with practice you know to how to balance this.

   Being a good rider, are you 100% protected from accidents? Nope, accidents can still occur but the probability is reduced as now you're in better control.

   Out of the above three INVESTMENT situations, two are bad.

But, if you set your qualification criteria right, you can save yourself with a lot of emotional dilemma and heartbreaks.

If you have set your qualification criteria right and you know you are with right women, even if the equation imbalances, it will be quite easy for you to push back again to the balanced situation.

The HOW becomes very easy if your WHY is clear.......

Similarly, it is essential to set the qualification criteria for your prospects in the **selling situation:**

As you strive to grow your sales, it's easy to get caught up chasing each and every lead that comes in your way. But all leads are not equal, some are more likely to turn into sales than others.

To avoid wasting precious resources, you need to strike out the long shots and concentrate your efforts on those leads who are likely to yield a return on your investment of energy, time and money.

The best way to qualify sales leads is N-E-C-B analysis.

Need - Emergency - Connect - Budget

NEED: If you don't know what your prospects need, how can you give them your best possible offer. This is an extremely critical process as if you don't understand the need or pain your prospects is facing at the moment; it will be effortless for you to pitch your product to them.

The key to need analysis is to ask open-ended questions and listen carefully.

This could be straight forward questions asking them

what problem they are facing at the moment. You can imagine yourself as a doctor in this situation and ask all possible, probable questions to go to the root cause in order to diagnose the pain. Ask What causes the pain, what elevates the pain, what are the elements of the pain.

To be a doctor, you need to yourself first understand and know thoroughly all essential functions of the body, disease, its treatment including medication, surgery if required and various therapies if needed. In other words, you need to be a SME (subject matter expert). Many prospective buyers know the pain but they themselves cannot see the source of the illness, or they may mistakenly think they know the source.

But you are an expert in your product or services, your clients are not. You have seen many companies/clients struggle with similar issues, where you have successfully addressed those issues and got results.

To tell you, if you ask the right questions, you may be able to help your clients find better solutions to their problems. In this case, chances are they will buy your services. As you no longer are a salesperson but a consultant, a problem solver, a real asset for the client.

You are not only offering a product/service, but helping your clients understand how to apply your product/service to meet a pressing need or to relieve their pain that may not have been fully understood by anyone before you.

With your experience you may even know what kind of people or organization may have the pain you can solve and setting those criteria helps you identify the list of right buyers and that will boost your sales number immediately.

EMERGENCY / URGENCY: Whenever you are in a selling situation, do you know what is common between, when you are transacting big with large corporates / governments or selling something small to an individual. The common fact is that you are dealing with Humans in both the scenarios and all humans behave the same , psychologically.

Psychologically, humans behave in the following two ways only:

- **Avoiding Pain (Bad consequences if delay in buying)**

  As humans, we tend to avoid negative consequences. This "loss aversion" means we'll do whatever it takes to prevent dangerous situations or any other negative outcome. The desire not to lose is often higher than the desire to gain.

  In sales, focusing on the penalties of not buying can have a significant effect on a customer's decision to buy. You may choose to illustrate how much money the customer could lose if he doesn't invest in your product/service, or how inefficient their business is and how flawed their current processes are. Whatever it is, focusing on the negative instead of the positive will have a psychological influence on your customers, which will lead them to the purchase decision faster.

- **Gaining Pleasure (Offers Benefits of Acting NOW)** Another motivating reason to act fast is to attain pleasure. We need to highlight to our prospect the joy they will get quickly from taking the decision on the buying offer. As a sales guy, you can add up the unique pleasure points (discount or offer to sales). Few examples of these offers can be a Package deal, Bundle offer, offer expiry date, Quantity Discount, Value Added deals, Seasonal / Festival / Periodic Offer, Prepayment Discounts.

  Both the above can be used in your discussion with clients to create urgency. Judge the urgency of the buying process and accelerate the buying process to create urgency.

CONNECT: You need to precisely identify all the key stakeholders in the sales process, as discussed in an earlier chapter. In the absence of a decision-maker in the loop or process, the sales will delay. You need to keep decision-makers in the loop. It has two strategies.

- **Bottom-up approach:** In this approach, you start your sales process with meeting the gatekeeper of the deal, then meet the influencer, then you get a chance to listen to the decision-maker. In this approach, you start from the bottom and go up, passing all the hurdles.

- **Top-Down Approach (Recommended)** This approach can be better for you to get results as you make your first contact with the top key holder. He will redirect you to staff down to take a look and report back to him.

In this strategy, you get better control over the process. One disadvantage of this approach could be that your product may be turned down at the very first instance but as per me sometimes getting "Bad news at an early stage is good News". Why because you save lots of time and energy in the process.

BUDGET:

Companies and people may have a desire and need to buy products and services. Still, on the level of spending money, this may be low on priority for them. Many people may want to buy a BMW or Mercedes, but the question is, do they have budgets for the same.

Talking about money may be a little awkward to talk to clients, and you may not know how the client will take it as well, how they will respond to these questions.'

Some tricky way to ask the question are given below: -

Q. What does your buying process look like, do you have budgets allocated to this project?

Q. Have you ever bought this kind of product or services earlier, if yes what price are you buying that?

Q. As we discussed, this problem is costing you and your team X amount today approximately, how are your budgets compared to these costs.

Q. Our product costs range between x to y, how will your budgets be against that?

Q. How much money it will take to build internally?

Q We can play around with price depending on the other terms you request. Approximately how much do you think [decision maker] wants to pay?

Q Would this be easier for you to push through if we [unbundled the package, billed you separately for X and Y, started on a lower rate]?

Price is a very very sensitive topic to discuss; please never give your final price. Always give your higher range and provide a hint that these prices are negotiable.

Don't put the same energy to all your options, instead prioritise!

CHAPTER
Seven

*Influence Customers,
they are always biased*

> *"People do not care how much you know until*
> *they know how much you care."*
> — *Theodore Roosevelt*

Whether it is a sales situation or intimate relationship, you are dealing with people. People are the same as they behave psychology.

You win a relation or a sales order not only because you are better than others but because people are biased about you somewhere in the corner of their heart unknowingly. This happens purely because of the rapport building.

Few quick ways to build rapport with anyone, these are based on root theory: **"People like people who are exactly like them or they would want to be like them."**

Use below tricks to get effective rapport building:

Eye Contact: Learn to look into her eyes and speak, have a warm, friendly and soft look into the eyes. So, you must be wondering what warm, friendly and delicate look are.

To give you an idea, laugh it loud, laugh hard. Now feel the area around eyes relaxed that is what is warm, friendly and soft eye contact. This is the same kind of eye contact that attracts women or anyone. Rule number 1 always have eye contact and do not lose eye contact because that's the sign of loss in interest.

Body Language: Observe the other person, how this person is sitting or standing, mirror them the way their body language is. To clarify this, please understand that people have three kinds of body posture,

- ***Equally distributed and strong*** (The way Army guys stand or sit), If you put the center line vertically from between the eyes from head to toe, the body would be equally distributed.
    - ▷ These are highly ordered and process-oriented.
    - ▷ They are good followers of structures
    - ▷ They always look for safety and security
    - ▷ Punctual on time
- ***Slight Disproportion:*** If you put the vertical line between eyes from head to toe, the person sitting or standing would be slightly disproportion.
    - ▷ They think of a win-win situation
    - ▷ These are benefit-oriented
    - ▷ Love showing off
    - ▷ Love brands
- ***Highly Disproportionate:*** If you put the vertical line between eyes from head to toe the person sitting or standing would be highly disproportion.
    - ▷ They are impulsive and quick decision-makers
    - ▷ They will go opposite to the structured way
    - ▷ They like to be appreciated
    - ▷ They are risk-takers

> ▷ Some have rebel characteristics
> ▷ Very harsh or straight forward in speaking

Look at the shoulders, are they straight up or bend down a little. How are their lower back, relaxed and comfortably round or straight, do they lay back on the chair or sitting without support. How are the legs and hands?

The rule is simple: just mirror the way they are standing or sitting, do it subtly, so they do not make this out, and do not be very obvious while doing it.

Facial Expressions Have relaxed and positive facial expressions. When listening to someone talking, keep nodding your head in a way that you are listening. Get yourself involved in the discussion and react appropriately without cutting the discussion in between.

When someone is conversing with you and in return, he wants to know whether you are with him in the discussion, which makes it two-way valuable communication. Keep nodding your head or keep saying yes/ok/wow/oh, depending on the expression required.

Appreciation: Whatever you appreciate in your life that grows. Appreciation can be an excellent tool to build rapport.

Don't fake the appreciation, as everyone understands when you are faking it.

If you look and listen deeply, you will find the right things to appreciate as everyone has some good stuff in them to be appreciated. We all want to be surrounded by people who like us and love us.

Appreciation is the way to let them know you like them; just don't overdo it and be genuine about it.

Open-Ended Questions: People deep down love talking, and they never get patient ears to talk it all they want. We just need to dig the other person so they can talk it all.

Open-ended questions which will have long answers. Knit the next open-ended question from the first answer that will lead you layer by layer inside another person. Listening passionately is the key.

Let me share a few examples of open-ended questions:

- What places should I visit in the city?
- What are your hobbies, and how did you get them?
- How do you generally spend your weekends?
- What are some good shopping places in the city?

Intersections: In the discussions find common areas of interest to keep the discussion and actions interesting. When people find common topics to talk, they passionately share that creates an invisible bond between them. When you ask open-ended questions, keep the focus on them and try to find out the interest and liking of another person.

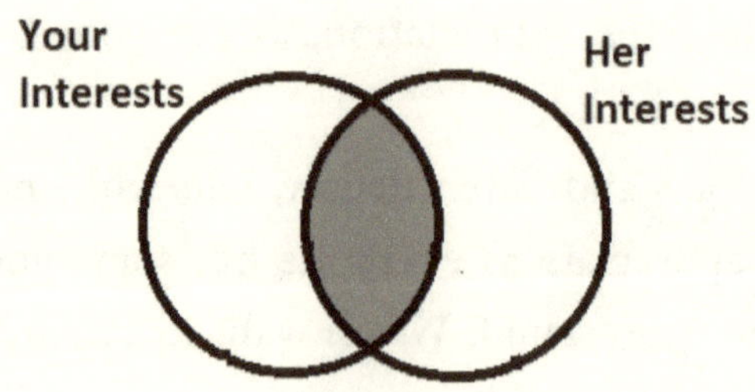

Laugh a Little: A good sense of humour is another essential skill to practice and excel. We all live in a very stressful environment, and if someone makes us stress-free, we would like to connect to that person again.

Little laugh is suitable for any rapport building relationship. Light moments, lots of smiles and finding a way to have friendly conversation are the key to success in dating.

Word of caution is don't overdo it otherwise you will be labelled as the funny guy in the group. When there is a serious discussion, and the context of the outcome of discussion requires you to be serious, don't get your sense of humour.

In the sales scenarios also adding a little sense of humour and many smiles make the discussion casual. This ease will help you get many clues in the deal cracking.

Homework: We have been given lots of homework in school, and homework makes us very powerful. Do thorough research on the person you are meeting.

Check their Facebook / Instagram / LinkedIn profiles, read if they have written any blogs. These activities will give you some threads to build upon.

Homework will give you lots of clues of intersections you could be ready with and use this in your interaction and discussion. It may also tell you a lot of common connections that could also be very handy to and can get the trust transferred from those people.

Be Genuine: Our mind is a powerful device, and it can sense the vibrations not from the talks, or from the way we look but from the from energy levels. It can quickly identify in the first few minutes of the discussion of how genuine is another person.

Authenticity comes with truth and honesty. Be the person people rely on. Honesty requires courage and a willingness to take a chance. It involves diplomacy and wisdom – and you must understand the conditions that make different people more receptive to truth.

Be the Icebreaker: We are social animals, and we love connecting and interacting with others, even with strangers. But many of us don't want to initiate the discussion because of our past experiences, our beliefs or literally because no one has taught us how to begin the conversation. Be the ICE breaker and go ahead and start the discussion with anyone. People love to discuss if someone comes and initiates the conversation with them.

First Impression: How to make a lasting first impression is a key to success. I believe whether a person will like you or not, it will be decided in the first 7 seconds of the discussion.

Let me tell you a secret to do that effectively; Imagine that you are meeting your very old and close friend after many years, how will you start the conversation, I want you to visualize the same energy levels, happiness and excitement.

If you use that same level of enthusiasm with strangers, you will have a charismatic first impression. In the first 7 seconds, another person does not focus on words but rather unknowingly focuses on energy levels. If you know how to create the best levels of energies, you are a winner.

Don'ts of Rapport building

- Never ever discuss politics to build the rapport as people may have very different political views than yours. You are fortunate, if your opinion matches with the other person. But if, it didn't meet then it may be very harmful to rapport building.

- Same is true for religion, never discuss religion with people as it may be very damaging because of the same reason given above.

- Never ask close-ended questions in the process of rapport building.

- Don't keep talking about yourself all the time.

- Don't be creepy or too sticky.

- Don't force other people to talk to; it has to be natural. Many people don't want to talk, and some people find casual conversation stressful, annoying, or inefficient.

- Don't disengage yourself in the discussion. If you're not interested in what your prospect / she is saying, it doesn't matter whether you both lived upon the same street growing up or obsess about the same

> obscure band: Your efforts to build rapport probably won't work.

- Never Argue, you may win an argument, but you lose the relationship.

- You are not practicing enough, Rapport-building is a skill just like any other — which means the more you practice, the better you'll get.

Suggestology (keep your senses open to sense what's next) We have five visible senses and one very powerful invisible sense called 6th sense or gut feeling. We have never learned to work in full balance and coordination of all together. We tend to majorly believe in what we hear or see not in coordination with all other senses.

Suggestology is the process of observation in which the other person gives us obvious clues on what should be done.

There are two ways of following the process:

- You follow the process as per your experience or on set rules and may not get through in the process.

- You follow the process as per your experience but not on set rules. You look for suggestions from other person and follow the procedure as per suggestions.

One thing we all have to keep in mind is that the entire process is happening for another person, and he or she is brilliant.

Brilliance is in the listener; it gives you signals what they are looking for but are you listening from all senses.

Suggestology has a few crucial parameters to look for:

Body Language: People can hide their feelings when they speak, but their bodies cannot hide their feelings. I hope you have heard Shakira *"Hips don't lie"* let me write my favourite lines of lyrics here.

Shakira, Shakira

Oh, baby, when you talk like that

You make a woman go mad

So be wise and keep on

Reading the signs of my body

I'm on tonight

You know my hips don't lie

And I'm starting to feel it's right

All the attraction, the tension

Don't you see, baby, this is perfection?

I am also saying the same, so be wise and keep on reading the signs of the body as the body never lies.

The most excellent sales guys, coaches and trainers look at body signs. How to look for body signs.

Look at facial expressions, shoulder movement, leg movement, the tension on the forehead, movement of eyes, movement of hands, look at lips. These body parts will give far greater information that even the other person is also not aware of.

Reading is an art, keep practising wherever you are.

When you are waiting at the airport, railway station or bus stand, try to read the body language of people around and become active observer. Once you learn this skill, you will become best at the art of persuasion.

Words

Words clearly show a frame of mind; we use specific terms because of a particular frame of mind.

We need to observe the use of words very carefully.

Even if you or others are joking or having fun, observations of the use of words are essential. Afterwards people might say "ooh I was joking" but even though while joking also why only those specific words.

Let me touch upon a little bit on word mind correlation.

People minds are of three kinds, and their words reflect their kind:

VAK (Visual / Auditory /Kinesthetic)

So, in our mind, we store information as one of the types majorly.

Some people store information in Images,

Some store information as they listen,

Some store as they feel.

Why is this important to understand?

If someone stores the information as Visual and the way you speak is Auditory, then it is as good as going to Spain and talking to people in Hindi. They listen, they may nod, but they will not understand.

So, if someone is visual, you get to speak with them using visual words.

Let them give you an example to make this clear; I will be writing the same meaning in 3 different ways. You try to judge VAK.

Example 1

1) Before you spoke to me, I was in the dark, and now I can see

2) As you spoke to me, I heard what you were saying

3) You provided me with a way to make sense of things

Example 2

1) The way I look at this is that it is still rather unclear.

2) I don't feel comfortable with this.

3) This doesn't sound right to me.

In both examples, the meaning of the sentence is the same, But the words are defining the frame of mind.

Let's confirm with you guess

Example 1

1) Before you spoke to me, I was in the dark, and now I can see (Visual)

2) As you spoke to me, I heard what you were saying (Auditory)

3) You provided me with a way to make sense of things (Kinesthetics)

Example 2

1 The way I look at this is that it is still rather unclear. (Visual)

2 I don't feel comfortable with this. (Kinesthetics)

3 This doesn't sound right to me. (Auditory)

Look at what words people are using. It will give you higher power to communicate effectively as well as it will provide you with suggestions on WHAT'S NEXT!

Be an Active Listener.

Environment

The specific selection of the environment also says a lot. It gives you an idea about the kind of person he is. Look at the surroundings very precisely if you are visiting some office, look at the details of the place, selection of things in the office, the way table is arranged, the way reception is arranged etc.

Few clues to see on the table when you are meeting them.

- If they have a picture of a family on the desk
- If they have a picture of God on the desk
- If the desk is perfectly organized.
- If the desk has a pile of paper and files
- If the desk has some toys/puzzles
- I the desk is not clean and messy
- If there is a bottle of hand sanitizer on the table

- What kind of coffee mug is on the desk?
- What kind of watch is in the room?
- Is there any flower vase in the room?
- Are there any awards or certificates in the room?
- Are there many sticky notes everywhere?
- Are there any inspiration posters in the room?
- Is the desk empty

Selection of place and arrangement of the place also talks a lot about the state of mind of the person and suggests to you a lot about your NEXT STEP!

ASK ASK ASK

The key to wisdom is knowing all the right questions at the right time!

If someone knows the right question, he will get what he needs. Asking the right questions gets you to the right places.

Questions trigger ideas, a great sales guys know how to ask the right questions and those answers helps him to define a clear next path.

If the client knew the right questions to ask for, they wouldn't be coming to you!

Our job as sales personnel is to help the client discover the right questions because the right questions will guide them to the correct answers.

Using the right question with the above techniques will help you guide and see what other people are thinking in their mind.

How to use suggestology in a Sales or Dating scenario?

These concepts of suggestology can be fundamental to learn and practice in dating or sales scenarios.

If I give you the power to read others' minds, then how powerful a sales guy will you become?

If with the same mind-reading power, you can read the mind of every girl in this world. Tell me will it be difficult to date successfully a girl?

I call suggestology the power of mind-reading.

Understanding and mastering these concepts are as good as creating a GPS for you to track people's mind. This is the crux of mind reading; mind reading can be straightforward.

Humans have created the language to speak and communicate. Still, no language can help us communicate precisely the same as what we are thinking.

In most cases, we are unable to make others feel the same as we think. I feel this is the biggest issue in the world today. It is difficult as the words are not enough as well words and their meanings have minor subjective differences the way we understand.

As a persuasive person, you use suggestology techniques in any situation and read the un-said. You can make people do what you want.

First Impression is a Lasting Impression (Not Last)

"When confused about what to wear,
always overdress a little."
– Kailash Pinjani

How we wear our clothes, makes an impression or perception. I have been always a big believer of, "Reality is not reality, Perception is reality."

First impressions are not only created when you meet someone. It can be created when you speak to someone on the phone or chat with someone for the first time.

Most of us behave the way we have been behaving since childhood, not realizing that it is making or breaking us.

Let me share some crucial parameters to have remarkable first impressions:

Right Attire, When I teach people the importance of first impression through proper dressing, some argue with me that we should be wearing what's comfortable and why we should think about others. I say if you feel comfortable in a night-suit (for some no suit is the best night-suit), will you wear a night-suit for important meetings or your birthday.

Whether you care or not others will have an impression of you from your clothes.

We, humans, have a very profound psychological condition called the halo effect. I call it psychological biases, as we always make an impression of another person in our first meeting in a fraction of a second. These first impressions are long-lasting and difficult to remove or change.

A simplified example of the halo effect is when an individual thinks that the other person in the photograph is attractive, well-groomed, and adequately attired assumes this person is kind, intelligent and awesome because the way he looks.

It can also be called an error in judgement as we just glance on one or two physical parameters and scores him high on rest of the other parameters.

We can use this halo effect in our favour. Do you want to know how?

It is very simple, wear right attire, groom well, and have command over language. You will create impressive and fantastic first impression.

Smile, when you meet someone. While talking, people will notice your your face and facial expressions. Smile is a god-given ornament that beautifies us. Have a sweet smile when speaking.

Keep your lips clean and soft with proper care. Keep your moustache trimmed. Have clean teeth, if you have issues with your teeth. Go and meet the dentist. Don't eat gutka and tobacco as it gives bad breath.

Start every conversation with a smile and practice smiling as much as possible.

Avoid having fake or plastic smiles and make sure not to overdo it.

Handshake, We shake hands when we meet someone for the first time. A handshake says a lot about our personalities.

Handshakes should always be firm.

I have seen lots of people doing wrong handshakes…

Dead fish Handshake: A lot of people do handshakes as if they have to hand over a dead fish to another person.

Crusher Handshake: A lot of people, do handshakes as they will crush another person's hand.

Overpowering handshake: A lot of people will handshake and keep their hand up. To keep their hand up, they will twist the hand of another person below.

Earthquaker: A lot of people shake the other person's hand too much as if they want to pluck the hand out of their shoulder.

Long Shake: Some people do not leave the hand and keep shaking the hand for long, this is called long shake.

Wet handshake: In few cases I have seen people doing wet handshake as their hand is wet. Their hands could be wet with water or sweat. Wipe your hands before handshake, if not possible to wipe then do not do it.

What is the right handshake?

The right way is that you hold the hand firmly. The firmness of your hand also depends on the other person's gender. If you are handshaking with a female, it has to be a little softer than the firm. And the hand should be left in 3-5 seconds.

Eye Contact: The eyes are more exact witnesses than the ears.

What is eye contact?

When you are meeting someone for the first time, where are your eyes moving or focusing?

Eye to eye contact is the best way of communication. Have confident and intense eye contact in business meetings. If you want to impress another person, have friendly vibes and smile with your eyes. Especially when you are talking to women, make sure you have firm eye contact.

Don't stare, have creepy expressions or run your eyes with lust, which will make women uncomfortable.

Eye contact can be the first step to knowing if a girl is interested in you. If you hold eye contact with a girl for more than a second or two (or if the girl looks at you, looks away, then looks back at you), it's a sign the girl is interested. So, after making eye contact with a woman, obey the two-second rule and talk to her within two seconds.

CHAPTER
Eight

Courage to Date -
Pitch yourself to fail

"Fail early, fail often, but always fail forward."
— *John C. Maxwell*

Fail Fast, Fail Often," is a quote used frequently among entrepreneur and business owners community. When you are running a company, it's best to "fail quickly and often" before actually succeeding.

Coincidently, this is also what the dating scene is. You must go on many dates, for a short period and "'fail fast" before you find the right "one."

I'm a big follower of the "Fail Fast, Fail Often" mindset, especially when it comes to dating or sales. For instance, I've gone on many dates/meetings where I just know that it's not going to work out.

Most of us live our lives in our heads and don't confront to our biggest fears.

Let me tell you the truth with my experiences that 95% of our fears are false and will never occur. You know why this happens, this has become part of our core psychological system to save us from troubles and keep us safe.

We will never grow or achieve our dreams with comfort; growth is a process of discomfort.

When a mother decides to give birth to a child, she has to go through lots of pain for nine months and after that. You cannot bring a child to this world without going through that pain.

In the dating scenario also, we need to accept that there could be pain after the final proposal, but that's the process of growth.

Let me tell you two scenarios....

1. You like a girl. You have done everything to make sure that the person internally knows or has a hint that you like her.

    You have never confronted that, and you have fear of failure or have your own limiting beliefs that she will reject you for XYZ bullshit reasons, and you never propose to her.

2. You like a girl. You have done everything to make sure that the person internally knows or has a hint that you like her.

    You have never confronted that, and you may be afraid of failure or have your own limiting beliefs that she will reject you for XYZ bullshit reasons. But still you want to propose her and keep your judgments aside and be prepared to listen to the real truth from her.

Let me tell you that you must be going through situation one right now or have gone through it sometime in your life,

Never live with regrets in your life, never live a life of "could have and would have" / "What if I could have asked, I may have received".

Living the life, you regret is more painful than living the life of temporary failure.

Never assume things or be judgmental about others perspective, get your doubts clarified.

There are a few things to keep in mind when you are preparing to dare.

- Make sure you have followed everything said in earlier chapters.
- However desperate you are inside, never look like one. Desperation is the key to failure in dating or sales.
- Pitch yourself well with high standards and just wait.
- Show the real value before the pitch.

If it is yours, it will find a way to reach you, if it is not yours, it will slip away. You have to try your best before letting it go because as Rumi says **"What you seek is seeking you."**

Before deciding to walk forward, learn to listen between the lines. Let me share another way to listen to things that are not said but are there for you.

Learning to read between the lines is learning to acquire superpower, you can know what is going on inside the person's mind.

See some examples

- You tell her that I am coming to your house to meet you, she says no, don't come. I have my family at home.

  ▷ Most people will understand that she doesn't want to meet me.

  ▷ I will give you a different perspective. She is happy to meet you, but her house is not the right place as she doesn't feel comfortable at the moment of being public. My next question should be, what is the right place?

- Sometimes you hold her hand, and she snatches her hand and says SOMEONE WILL SEE don't do it.

  ▷ Most people will understand that she doesn't like me and does not want me to hold her hand.

  ▷ I will give you a different perspective. She may like me to hold her hand, but this place is not right, and the time is not correct.

Don't be too pressing and if you are getting the same message, again and again, you are not reading it correctly.

Humans have psychological errors to see what they want to see. There is a massive difference between reading between the lines and seeing what they want to see. You have to be careful not to read between the lines to satisfy your hope.

Give another person a chance to take few steps forward; this will only happen when you give another person a chance to do that, and there is a small pause from your side.

The pause will give her a chance to evaluate and deep down find you inside her. Beware this pause may also become the full stop in some relationship, but that's the real test.

As I say dare to Courage and pitch yourself to fail.

Same is true for sales and prospecting...

Biggest mistake sales guys or you are making today is that you are too desperate for results. Success in selling comes from the right balance of asking for a close but not being too desperate to close.

A lot of sales executives ask me that we have targets and quotas to achieve, we have review meetings every morning and we have to project and bring the sales, and we become desperate unknowingly. How do we handle this situation? How can we not be desperate?

The answer to not being very desperate is straightforward in a sales situation than dating, but the answer to both is the same.

Have a backup plan ready to jump on, what I mean by this is you have sales quotas to achieve, and you are answerable to your performance, you have two ways of handling the situation:

1. Keep pressing the few right prospects you have to close and be desperate, keep losing sales and live in stressful situations.

2. Keep plan B ready and keep working on that as well, so you know that you have a longer pipeline than expected.

So even if your best bet doesn't close you have another case to back it up. This will give you the power to be not desperate and be cool and in control over the situation. This is a mental game than a real game.

Plan B just gives you mental peace, and this peace will provide you with a higher power to close the best bets as you are in control.

Same is true for dating as well, but don't go around keeping dating multiple women. Just keep your back plan ready, so it gives mental peace and not too desperate.

I have seen some terrific sales guys who are good at the process, but they are not good at closing or not able to help clients to make decisions.

If you do everything in the sales process and leave closing in the hands of clients, then your chance of winning the order is very, very low.

I see lots of sales guys and entrepreneurs who do everything in the sales process but don't know how to close. Those are the one not getting results or not liking the sales process. Results keep you motivated and keep you on the track.

The great sales guys know how to close.

What is Sales Closure?

Sales closure is the process when the entire process of sales moves to the transaction of money in exchange for value. A good sales closure is a win-win situation where buyer is happy with the value, he/she is getting in return of money they are paying. The seller is also happy with the money he is getting in exchange of product/services.

The main aim of the sales process is to achieve this end so called the orgasm of the process. Well achieved orgasms make both the parties want to do the process again and again and well-done sales closure will give high to both the parties and they would like to repeat the same sales process again and again.

In theory the entire sales process from the start till the end is a simple process. But the sale's closure becomes a bit complicated when after the whole progression the customer starts avoiding you, stating that he doesn't want to buy or he doesn't buy from you.

You arrive at a situation where sales closure does not materialize, your entire effort, your invested time goes on the toss, you lose on your sales quota, company losses the sales target and your loose commission or incentives.

I find most sales guys fail to do sales closures. They do their best but leave closing for customers to decide.

For customers, this is one of the deals, and they are not expert judging the value of your product and services in depth against your competition.

In closures, not the best product or best company wins, it is the best sales guy backed up with the right product or company wins.

20 Modern-Day Sales Closing Techniques to Close More Deals

1. The Assumptive Close
2. The Take Away Close
3. The Now or Never Close
4. The Summary Close
5. Something for Nothing Close
6. The Objection Close
7. The Pros & Cons Close
8. The Challenge Close
9. The Need Close
10. The Scale Close
11. The Visual Close
12. The Empathy Close
13. The Artisan Close
14. The Alternative Close
15. The Opportunity Cost Close
16. The Ownership Close
17. The 'Best Time to' Close
18. The Calendar Close
19. The Testimonial Close
20. The Thermometer Close

The Assumptive Close

This is an effortless closing technique, as the name suggests you assume the sale is close and the deal has been made. You can use this technique when everything above is done and just simply ask when can we start.

The Take Away Close

Threaten to take away the deal, and you'll see how well they behave now.

This works perfectly with few prospects.

You're about to close the deal, but your customer is unwilling to proceed. He/she has suddenly come up with issues to do a bargain. An immature sales guy here would fulfil all their offer and complaints whatever customer ask just for the desperation of closing the deal. Instead, an experienced sales guy wouldn't give away things easily.

Use the Take Away closing technique in the situation; you can offer to withdraw the whole deal and move out from the customer to push them to accept your offer. This technique can be used for those who happen to be taking lots of time with little progress.

The reason is that letting go of your client shows how confident you are in your product, which then gets them to reconsider the excellent product that he/she may be missing out.

The Now or Never Close

Urgency creation is also important to close deals faster. The Now or Never Close is a technique where you put pressure on the prospect to make a quick decision. This technique works when coupled with a freebie for a limited period or special discount.

This technique is used when the customer is on the phone to buy your product. Like the Take Away Close technique, a sense of urgency comes into play and the fear of missing out (FOMO) on discount nudges the prospect to get your product.

The Summary Close

Think of a closing argument given by an advocate in a court. There are no new concerns or facts introduced here. Just an act of selectively summarising the highlights and value propositions and pointing towards the only logical conclusion that emerges from connecting the dots that help customers to close.

The Summary close works excellent when you have gone through an extensive evaluation/discussion over some time, and it is time to switch top gears.

Something for Nothing Close

Humans are inclined to return good act.

We all have heard of Givers-Gain rule; givers always gain in return.

The Something for Nothing Closing works around this rule. You give your prospective buyer an extra feature or free add-on in goodwill or to take away some of the work they will have to do or pay extra to get it done, and they'll be obligated to do something in return – that something can be buying the product.

This works because people like free things that eases their work or are complementing to what they are buying. But the freebie you give should be of value to them and less cost to you.

The Objection Close

This is a compelling technique as the prospect is giving you exact reason not to close and that indirectly means if you sole their objections, then they will close. Do ask and check if these objections are taken care will they move forward.

Once you have done an excellent job that your prospect has understood everything about your product or service and what it has to offer, try asking them for any objections they might have with the product.

The Pros & Cons Close

Listing down the pros and cons of your product or services in comparison with your competition. This will help the prospect visualise how valuable your product or services can be for them. It's best used when the candidate is confused whether to buy your product or not, you can make a list of the pros and cons, and once they see that the advantages outweigh the disadvantages, the odds of closing the deal improves.

The Challenge Close

The Challenge Closing Technique is best used when the prospect is most likely going to buy your product, but they have one objection that is stopping them. They bring the opposition like 'can you deliver' or 'there is an issue' or so on. Using this tactic, you can answer this with another relevant question to close the deal.

If you get a positive response, the deal is done. If you get a negative reply, you know that either there is some issue or they're not serious. Here you have a second chance to clarify any other questions they have.

The Needs Close

Satisfying a prospect's exact needs is the best way to get them to buy your product or service, and that's what the Needs Close technique does. First, list the things the customer said they needed from your product, prioritise burning needs. Then review the list against your product/ service and start ticking off the ones that match. The more boxes ticked, the better is the product/service for the customer.

The Needs Close technique works in situations where the customer is not able to visualise how your product could benefit them. By listing and ticking off the matching ones, you are showing the customer how your product is helping them.

The Scale Close

Sales Rep: *"On a scale of 1 to 10, how interested are you in our product?"*

Prospect: *"I'd say an 8.*

Sales Rep: *"Wow! Great. Just curious, why an 8?"*

Prospect: *"I love your X, Y, Z features and I have a feeling those are going to help our company the most.*

Sales Rep: *"Most of our customers love them. And these are some great reasons, but I'm curious why it's not a 10."*

Prospect: *"Despite your product having great features, we feel that it's too pricey."*

Sales Rep: *"I agree. But when you use our product, you will get to know that the ROI on the product will be so clear that the cost would barely matter. We never had an existing customer come back and complain about the price."*

Sometimes everything looks good, but the prospect is not moving forward and does not have objections. It's best to approach them with the 'On the scale of 1-10' line.

Based on their rating, you can either clarify their objections if the score is low or proceed to close the deal if they give you a high score. This will help you analyse the customer's interests and gives you a chance to solve any concerns they might have.

The Visual Close

"These past few months have brought some fruitful conversations between us, and I've appreciated the effort and time you have put into this. I hope you feel the same way. Ever since we have reached out to you, this is how far we have come..."

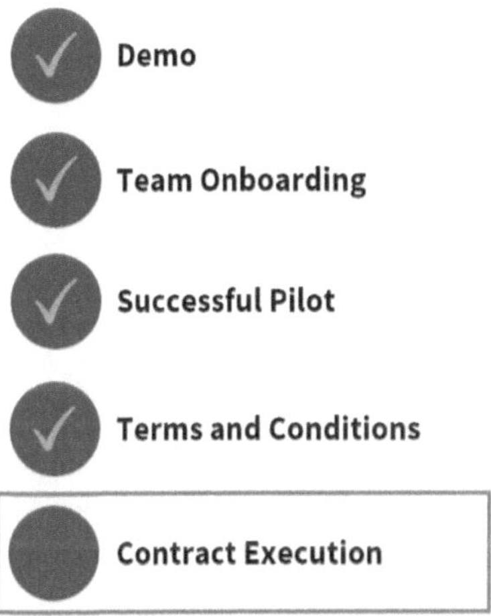

"Here is good news. We have completed all the steps required to make sure you can use our product/service effectively. All that is left is to put pen to paper and bring this thing home?"

Using visual aids such as charts, videos or even table with the pros and cons listed, you can attractively close deals. The Visual Close sales technique is quite popular among sales guys because it appeals to a customer's visual perception, and as we all know, *a picture is worth 1000 words.*

It's easier for the customer to visualise what you're trying to put forth.

The Empathy Close

Not every deal has to be closed using pressure or leverage. Sometimes it's good to take the empathy path.

The Empathy Closing sales technique allows you to use emotion to understand the situation of your customer. When the customer tells you that he/she isn't ready to make a decision, it's sometimes useful to give them more time to think rather than pushing for a close.

Empathising with your customers can help build a special bond with the customer, which can be useful in the long run.

The Artisan Close:

The Artisan Closing sales technique lets you highlight the amount of work, skill, and time that is being invested in the product. It will create the value you are trying to bring on the table and efforts you are putting into making sure the experience is perfect. It deviates from the usual sales technique norms by focusing more on behind the scenes of your service/product, rather than the prospect or the benefits of your service/product.

This technique works best with customers who are appreciative of something that has a lot of effort and hard work put into it.

The Alternative Close

The Alternative Close is a variant of the Assumption close, where you assume that the customers are interested in your service/product, and you provide them with two choices that will move the deal further.

Whatever choice they choose, it should help you take a step towards the closing.

This technique works best with customers who don't have any queries on your service/product or any objection with the features, price, etc.

Why is it useful?

By giving them choices, you simplify the decision-making process and get them to commit to your service/product.

The Opportunity Cost Close

In business terms, the Opportunity cost is the cost of forgoing something. That is the cost you incur by not doing something. This technique taps into the same principle by stressing on what the customer will miss if they don't implement your solution.

When using the Opportunity Cost technique, insist why purchasing your product is not an expenditure but rather an investment – highlight the ROI they will enjoy such as saving time, better efficiency etc. which are more valuable in the long run, compared with the what they'll spend on your product.

The idea is to make the customers realise that the longer they take to purchase, the more they'll stand to lose.

The Ownership Close

Have you ever come across one of those car salesmen who make a sales pitch talking as you already own the vehicle – Asking like, if your garage needs a rework or how frequently you plan to go on a road trip etc.

Classic Ownership close technique; where the seller places the idea of the buyer owning the product.

Using this, you paint a picture in the customer's mind, that his business will change for the better; being a hypothesis, this strategy works when backed up with facts that show how their key metrics will improve once they purchase your product – Tell stories of terms goals achieved, competitions crushed etc. that will make the customer jump in and start using your product immediately.

By repeatedly stating the benefits they will enjoy, you create a mental closure that your product will improve their business, thus making it easy for you to finalise a deal.

The 'Best Time to' Close

The 'Best Time to' close is beneficial when you notice there is a trigger event related to the prospect – you use the timely happening to persuade the customer, why now is the right time to invest in your product:

Examples:

Is the customer expanding their business?

Did one of their competitors just secure a new round of funding? Or

Are you having a Diwali sale with huge discounts?

You relate the timely happening with your service/product and put convincing statements like why it is the best time to purchase.

The Calendar Close

There will be some customers who will be on the fence when it comes to signing the deal.

You can't wait forever for them to make up their mind, and at the same time, you cannot give up on them either, because they are almost near to the closing line.

So, what do you do, in that case?

You suggest a date in the near future to finalise the deal.

This way, you eliminate the hassles of back and forth exchanges and fix a timeframe by which the customer should come to a decision.

Based on their response, you can also identify the level of commitment of the customer in signing a deal.

The Testimonial Close

The Testimonial close is a powerful sales technique which helps you build trust and credibility with customer, which are the critical factors for any business relationship.

When using this technique, instead of talking about the product yourself, you can share the experiences of actual users who have benefitted from your product.

Testimonials are beneficial because they come from people who have used the product and fell in love with it – their opinions are neutral, genuine and free from any bias.

The other reason why this technique works is that when you share the success stories of your existing users, you ease your customer's concerns and doubts on whether your product can help achieve their business goals.

The Thermometer Close

The Thermometer close is a great technique to identify and overcome the objections that your customer might have, which is keeping the deal from moving forward and gauging how close they are to making a purchase.

Using this, you give the customers a scale of 1 to 10 and ask them to provide a score on how likely they are to purchase your product.

If the customer responds with a score of 6 or lower, then it means that they have an objection that you need to address to proceed further.

On the other hand, if they give a score between 6 and 10, then they understand the value your product brings but still have a few doubts that you may probably need to clarify.

When using the Thermometer Close, the objective is to make the customer give you a score of 10, which means that they are ready to jump on board immediately; anything less than a perfect 10, is an indicator of objections that you need to overcome.

The goal is to repeat the process and address the objections, as many times as it takes until the prospect gives a 10.

Closing is an Art, and if you are willing to give a try, you will learn this effective technique to be a winner in life. What choice do you have if you don't learn this art? To be a successful sales guy, you may have to learn everything, but if you are not able to close clients, everything may go on a toss.

CHAPTER
Nine

The Art of Not Negotiating

"To win a negotiation, you have to show you're willing to walk away with peace and blessings."

What do you think negotiation is?

From childhood we have seen in our surroundings to learn negotiation, getting anything at the lowest possible cost is a good negotiation skill?

That's where we got wrong as our basics are wrong.

Let me explain to you why I say our basics are wrong. I want you to think of the same scenario from two different perspectives.

1. When you are a buyer, and you go to the seller and push them hard to give the product at lowest possible cost and if you can beat the last time purchased price you feel pleased about it.

2. Let's turn the tables, and now think that you are a seller. A customer comes to you and does a tough negotiation using his tricks. You end up giving the product or service at a lower than ever to this customer. How do you feel as a seller, terrible and after you take the money you crib this customer a lot?

Do you feel that your clients always negotiate very hard with you? Think if you are doing the same with your vendor.

What Goes Around Comes Around!

I have been learning to control the art of negotiating for a long time. I have attended many leaders' talks on negotiation, but all tricks went into vain. Then I realize the

The art of negotiating is Not Negotiating, still winning the order!

It is rather easy said than done. In this chapter, I will give lots of ideas and ways to do that.

The first reaction to a lot of people after hearing this will be: Is it possible?

Are you asking the same question? If yes then let clarify that it is 100% possible.

Have you been for a tea/coffee meeting at a 5-star hotel? What is unique about tea there? They charge Rs.500 for the same tea that is available outside the shop at Rs. 10.

Do you go and bargain and negotiate with the manager there and ask for a discount?

Let's say you ask for a discount and tell your client (with whom you are meeting there); "The hotel is cheating us, as Rs 500/- for just a cup of coffee is way too much. Let's get a low price from them. If you do what they will say, moreover what will your client say?"

Have you ever been to an Apple store to buy an iPhone or MAC, do you negotiate there and say the same features and functionality phone and computer are available on 30% lower cost, so you need a discount?

Have you gone to buy Bose headphones and asked why Bose is Rs 30,000, and negotiate there as headphones are available at Rs 500 also?

I know you must be thinking that they are Brands.

The rule of negotiation is that your client should feel embarrassed asking for a discount, if that is happening then you are becoming the brand.

That's how we say the real negotiation is not negotiating and continuously striving for becoming a brand.

Let's find out how to become a non-negotiable brand?

The first rule of a non-negotiable brand is to learn to walk out. Yes. Learn to walk out.

I know what you are thinking, how will we do sales and business if we start walking-out of our customers.

When you create the vacuum, the world will fill the vacuum with the right customers. To create the vacuum, you learn to walk out.

How to handle walking out on negotiating and continue growing: -

- Have your pipeline long enough that walking out of few customers does not create an issue (Read next chapter call The Magic Funnel)

- Have a marketing system in place, so you are adding new lead continuously. Your incoming leads are always higher than a walkout.

- Keep working on improving your brand value.

- Keep thinking about how can you give more value instead of reducing your product/service cost.

- Train your customer-facing team (front line team), that they can project right values to the prospective customer

- With time you will know who is your customer and who is not.

- Understand that every customer is not yours

One disadvantage you may feel is that once you become a fixed price company, your customers will not ask for a discount; instead, they will go and buy cheaper options. I feel that is an advantage as you are attracting right customers who will believe in quality and are brand conscious.

If you have been giving discounts to win customers for many years, then you need patience. This shift will create vacuum in your pipeline for some time, and cash flow will be an issue for you. You got to plan well for this vacuum time.

Plan gradual shifts, create segments of your customers as per products and services. Then plan segment by segment gradual upgradations.

Give 10X Value

Always remember to give 10X value and experience in the process of sales and post-sales support. When you continuously give 10X value, you will be a brand built on high value for customers.

The three soft parameters to create 10X value

1. **Become Authority**

   Once you become an authority in your field, your customers will feel that you're giving 10X. When your clients visit your company's website, and sees lots of positive reviews and testimonials, your customer will have a sense of trust for your product and services. Being authority gives your customer a great sense of security.

   Do you have a public domain on the internet where you have positive reviews from your customers?

   Is someone from your office closely monitoring that?

2. **Understand your Customers Better**

   When you start understanding your customers and listen to them better, it will create a connection between your company and the customer. This connection will give them value. In today's busy world, people do not give enough time to their customers. Brands are built on relations and relationships. If your customers feel like connecting to you and you love listening to them, this personal bond and connection will create 10X value.

3. **Surprise your Customers**

   If you are in personal business, ideally every business should create systems to make customer interaction personal. Remember your customers birthday, Anniversaries and surprise them with those dates. Surprise them with additional and personalized services you can create for them. When humans feel that you have done something out of the usual, or beyond the call of duty, your value shoots up. Remember with value comes loyalty.

Discount and Offers

Non-negotiable brands do not mean that you don't run discounts and offers for your customers.

You get to plan various incentives for your customers. This has to be static regardless of the customer asking or not.

In case you run a Cash Discount for customers who pay full in cash and advance, regardless of whether the customer is asking or not, he should be getting this discount.

If the last date of the offer is committed to the customer, follow that date seriously as they are looking at you. All of your actions should be transparent and similar across the customers.

Customers should feel everyone is treated the same.

These below are the discount and offers you can plan for your customers:

- **Cash Discount**

  These offers are created to generate a sense of urgency. These are generally time-bound offers. Like Month End Sale, Festival Offers etc. These offer 5% to 80% for your customer if they try to decide to purchase the offer immediately. If a customer walks away, he or she may lose the offer.

- **Bulk Purchase Discount**

  If a customer buys the same product in bulk, in multiple quantities, there should be levels of policies derived for these kinds of customers. In most corporate sales orders, the sale will come in bulk; they need special treatment from you. One thing to take care of is that post-sales services have to be customized as per their requirements.

- **Group Discount**

  Group Discount is similar to Bulk purchase; the only difference is that in the Bulk purchase same customer buys in bulk, but in group, customers will come as a group to buy your product in multiple quantities. While designing rules of this offer or post-sales service, take care that every customer is a separate customer.

- **Referral Discount**

  The customer refers you to the new customer. You should have a referral offer to this customer that can be used in the next purchase. This will encourage your customers to become the brand ambassador for your company, and they will keep referring new customers to you. The thing to remember is that they are not referring as they need a discount, but they love your company. You are giving them a token of appreciation.

- **Free Shipping**

In lot of cases, the product requires shipping. Sometimes weight, some time because of size and sometimes because of distance. Every shipping need customer to take a lot of pain and spend a lot of money. When you offer shipping, you not only take away the cost of shipping from the customer but also a lot of mental pain of arranging everything.

Keep Shipping and service time as low as possible.

- **Free Service for Next X Months**

In some services, you can run time-bound offers for your customers to take pending decisions going with your company. This offer gives customers reason to believe you immensely. You as a company are not thinking short rather long term. This connection helps your customer make quick decisions.

- **Value Added Offers**

You can create Value Added Offers to your main product. Your customer will require these value-added products, and they will have to rebuy it. You decide to give them a bundle at the same cost. That surprises your customer, and they are delighted.

- **Product Bundling offers**

  If your customer decides to buy your two or more products and services together, you ideally design a product bundle in a way that you cross-sell products and services together. Customers are tempted to buy more products as bundle offers are more lucrative than a single purchase.

Things to remember while designing the offers.

- These offers should be time-bound and follow these timelines strictly.

- Keep repeating these offers with a time gap.

- Your sales team should be highly trained to suggest the right offers to your customers.

- The offers should be transparent and should be available to all the customers.

- The offer should be given even if the customer does not need them.

- The offers should be designed keeping various customers segments and their buying behaviours.

- Keep analyzing the sales and discount feedback from customers, so you keep improvising.

Win-Win Approach

It is very important to create all the relationships in a Win-Win Situation. It is the principle of coexistence as you are there, so I am. If you grow, so do I grow. If you are happy, I will be. It is my responsibility to think good for you and me too.

It is the responsibility of the business owner as well as sales guys to make sure that Win-Win deals happen between customer and company.

Sometimes playing chess alone, when you are playing from the side of black you think of the advancing black, and when you are playing from the white side, you get to think of white's benefit.

So, when you are sitting in front of a client, you are thinking from the Company's perspective majorly. When you are talking to a company, you are speaking from the customer's side. The role of sales guys is to bridge the gap between customer and company.

Role of sales guys is to liaison between company and customer and get them both to have a mutually benefitting situation. This means as a sales guy, you not only negotiate terms with your clients but also from your company for customer's benefit.

The Peaceful Non-Negotiating Mind

I have a lot of gratitude for money mentors, Ken Honda from Tokyo Japan and Murali Sundaram from Chennai. My Money mentors taught me these principles. Thank you, for teaching me these principles.

How to become a Non-Negotiating Person (For Price)?

How to change the world around you, so they do not negotiate prices with you?

This is a fundamental principle of life, how many of you know that we are magnetic, and we attract everything that is happening to us and around us. You feel all of your customers are cribbing a lot on price and negotiate a lot. Whether you believe or not, you are attracting all those customers into your life.

In this part, I will discuss how to attract non-negotiating customers.

Isn't it amazing if you could attract every customer to your life who is not negotiating with you?

Do you want to know the secret of that?

Become that kind of customer first!

Let me clarify, so you understand this - How do you behave as a customer to your vendors?

Let me ask some more questions; you have to answer honestly.

Do you feel negotiation is your birthright?

Do you always crib your vendors and try your best strategies to pull their prices down?

When you do the negotiation and pull the prices down, do you feel very happy?

Do you feel the fixed prices shops are there to charge more?

When you go to the vegetable market, do you always negotiate from vegetable vendors, especially when you know that they are charging Rs 10 extra?

Do you always negotiate with rickshaw drivers when you use their service?

What places do you always negotiate at?

If even one of the answers to the above question is 'YES', then it is vital for you to read further.

People always treat you how they have been treated and not how they feel about you.

If you have been negotiated hard by customers, so you do the same to your vendors.

My question to you is how to break this vicious cycle of negotiation…

It is very simple, do what is in your control?

Two things are happening simultaneously. One you are negotiating with your vendors, and second, your customers are negotiating with you. Which one is in your control?

Yes, you have control over your vendor and your actions. Stop negotiating with your vendors. Find the right vendors who give fixed price. Learn to walk out of vendors who negotiate.

We have a lot of people on earth who don't negotiate, and they don't even check the price tag before buying. You will attract similar kinds of people to your life. If you behave the same way, then you will attract similar kind of people in your life as customers.

Why does this happen?

When you do not negotiate with your vendors, you walk out from your negotiating vendors. Because you genuinely believe that it is possible to have an excellent non-negotiating client as you an excellent example to your vendors.

This belief will give you power to create non negotiating conditions with your clients and walk out of negotiating clients.

> *"I attract to my life whatever I give my attention, energy and focus to, whether positive or negative."*
> *– Michael Losier*

I want you to implement this for 30 days and tell me the difference. Write to me on **kailashcpinjani@gmail.com**.

CHAPTER
Ten

The Magic Funnel of Success

> *"People do not buy goods and services. They buy*
> *relations, stories and magic."*
> – Seth Godin

After having tremendous experience as a Front Line Sales Executive to Vice President Sales for a global organization to running my own companies as an entrepreneur, I have realized that you need a brilliant **"System for Marketing and Sales"**.

What is a System?

The system is a repeatable process that gives the same results every time you run it in all conditions and circumstances. The system is fail-proof.

What is a System for Sales & Marketing?

It is difficult to understand how you can create a system for sales and marketing. If it is possible, then why do we need sales department in an organization?

The system is the design of the sales process that helps customers to float from one product to another product and service automatically. Role of the sales team is to facilitate the customer in smooth moving across the various products or services. So that those customers are happily associated with the organization for a long period of time.

Why do you need a System for Sales and Marketing?

For running a successful business, you need to keep

serving the customer with value. Ideally, that's the reason companies exist to add value in customers' lives. Customers are just exchanging money in return for the value you are adding to their life.

If you add value to a few people's life you are a small business, if you add value to a few thousands of people's lives, you are a small and medium business, and if you add value to millions of lives, you are a large business.

We all need customers every month, the more customers you are serving every month, the better your company is.

If you have a system to automate this process of bringing and winning customers every month, you soon become one of the largest company of your country and then of the world.

The most important world is **AUTOMATIC**.

Let's learn how to build the magic funnels for your company, your product and services.

You have to understand and find out a way to calculate below values approximately if not accurately: -

Customer Acquisition Cost (CAC)

Customer acquisition cost is the investment you do to acquire every new customer. You need to have accurate measurements to find that out every month.

To calculate the customer acquisition cost use the below formula.

$$CAC = \frac{\text{Spending in Sales \& Marketing}}{\text{Number of new customers Acquired}}$$

You need to have a clear tracking process to calculate both the parameters.

List of few items to be included in the calculation of spending Sales & Marketing

- Salaries of sales and marketing team

- Other expenses of the sales & marketing team

- Advertisement spends across various modes and channels

- Cost of creatives creation

- Approximate time management to handle new customers queries

- You can add anything that goes to acquire a new customer

You should also have a sales process to track how many new customers you are acquiring every month and also how many old customers are buying again.

This number can go up and down every month.

Customer Lifecycle Spend (CLS)

CLS is the spending customer does or can do with your company for all the products and services you offer. That means if the customer is associated with your organization then how many products and services the customer can buy from you during his association.

Let me give an example, so you get this very clearly…

Business to Customer Example for woman will understand better.

Let say you run a **Beauty parlour**, and you do marketing of your parlour services to attract women clients. If this new woman attaches to your parlour for a year, and let say the following two scenarios occurs:

Case 1: Lady will get the Waxing and Eyebrow every month and Facial every three months, Hair Cut every 6 months will spend minimum 15000/year with you.

Case 2: Lady will get the Waxing and Eyebrow every month and Facial every two months, Hair Cut 3 months, Make-up Twice a year, Hair straightening once a year will spend minimum 50000/year with your parlour.

So let's assume 3 years is the Customer Lifecycle Spend that is between 45,000 to 1,50,000 for you.

Business To Business Let me take an example in this case for everyone to understand

Let's say you are an owner of an **IT Hardware company**; Your company deals into computers, Laptops, Servers, Microsoft Software's, Anti Viruses, Backup Solutions etc. etc.

Once a new customer attaches to your company, they will give orders for all the above necessary products and software for 3 to 5 years.

The CLS will be between Rs. 1 Million to 10 Million depending on the size of the customer.

Business To Business Example for the service industry

Let's say you are an architect and provide your architectural services for your builders and construction companies. A mid-size builder will have 3-4 medium-sized projects (1 lakh square feet) every year and a big builder will do one massive project (350 acres to 400 acres) and 3-4 mid-size projects every year.

Once a new builder is attached to you and works with you for three years, your CLS will be between Rs. 1Million to Rs. 100Million.

I am giving very high emphasis for you to understand these principles as lots of business owners will never look at their business from these angles and judge customers from every transaction.

So, they will compare CAC with the first transaction only and not from CLS

Beauty Parlour owner will compare Investment in marketing with one lady who just got the haircut done and not consider the CLC which has INR 15000 to 1.5 Lakh potential.

The **IT hardware** company owner will compare Investment in marketing with one laptop, which a mid-size company recently bought.

An **Architect** will compare an investment in marketing with one small project that a builder has given them to execute.

We, as business owners always undervalue our customers as we just look at things from an individual transactional level.

If you know your CLS accurately, you will never shy away from marketing spends.

The Magic Funnel

The magic funnel has two principles in place.

1. Circle of trust
2. The Flow of Funnel

Circle of Trust

Your best customers were once strangers

We live our lives at the center, and we create a virtual circle around us. This circle is like a fence, people inside this fence will be known and trusted people, and outside of this fence are unknown or strangers.

Prospective Buyer

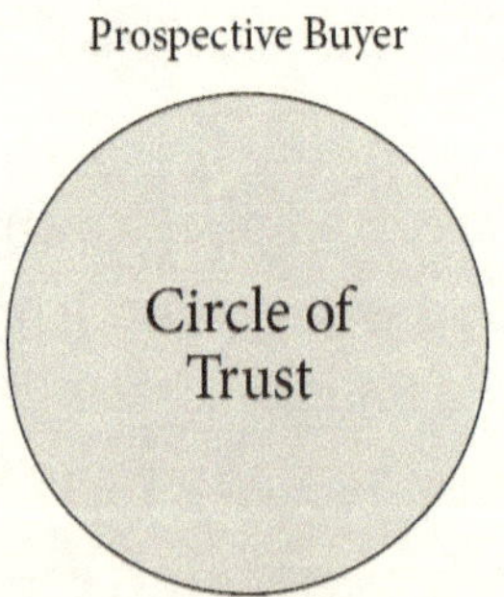

When you meet someone for the first time, they are strangers who are outside of our circle of trust.

Now the big question is, how can we get inside the circle of trust to make the long-lasting win-win relationships quickly.

Assume a scenario, that a senior sales executive who wants to become your trusted vendor is sitting in front of you for the very first time. He is a total stranger to you today.

What risks you would have if you decide to give the work to his organization.

What could be those quantifiable risks....

1. Risk of Time

2. Risk of Money

3. Risk of Emotions (Cannot be measured)

The same risk your customers are also experiencing when you or your sales team is sitting in front of them to start a new relationship. Unconsciously your prospective clients are also thinking about same risks in their mind.

What can you do to minimize or totally zero down the above three risks for you to start the relationship.

The answer is very simple:

- Reduce the risk of time to minimal

- Reduce the risk of money to as low as possible

- Reduce the risk of emotional loss to a minimum

As risks go down to minimal, it is very easy for other

people to start a new relationship with you. And then gradually you start progressing towards the center of the circle of trust.

Design your product and services in such a way that if new customers want to start an association with you, his above-mentioned risks are less. Reduce your boundaries so people can quickly jump to your service or products.

What can you do to design the less risky propositions, let me run through some ideas? I understand some of the ideas may not be logically fit in the industry you work for. We can have One to One meeting if you want me to help you personally. If you are just a trader and not the creator or manufacturer of your product, then it might be a little difficult but still possible.

Tangible

- Money-Back Guarantee
- Free Demo of Product
- Free Trial of few days or months
- Create a smaller version of products for forever free

Intangible

- High-Value Information related to you in industry
- Customer Testimonials
- Cross Networking

These risk-reducing ideas have to be personally designed as per your industry and specifically for your company.

The Magic Funnel

I would like to give credit of these Funnel learnings to Mr. Russel Brunson. I have learned these principles from the book Dotcom Secrets: The Underground Playbook for Growing Your Company Online with Sales Funnels. I highly recommend you to buy this book and learn these principles in depth.

I have applied these principles in my businesses, and my clients' businesses and all of these principles have always worked very well every time. Go ahead, read Russel's book and design for yourself or if you need my help in designing these Magic Funnels for your company, let me know.

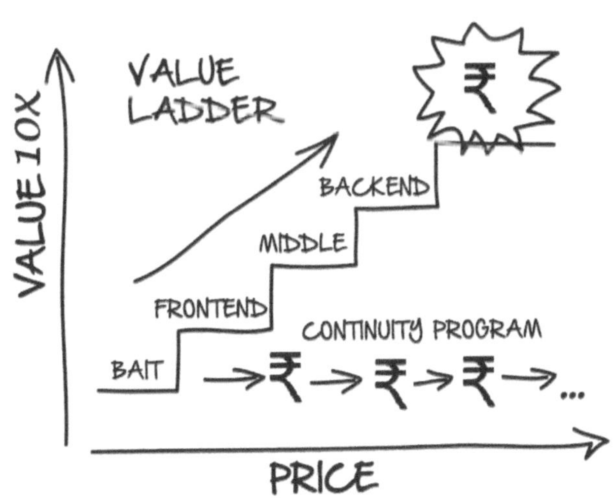

Image Credit: Mr Russell Brunson

The magic funnel is the process in which customers start interacting with you and start working in a very low-risk environment. Customers start gaining trust in your work and then move to the next level of product or service that is higher in value and price.

Bait is the smallest risk product/plan, always remember. The value you give is 10X, and in the process of providing value, you may lose some money in the transaction but always remember the Customer Life Cycle Spend. This is just an investment to acquire new customers.

One more thing to know that there is a lot of effort, time and money involved to create the bait product as we always believe in giving 10 X value.

Once a client is happy with bait and feels tremendous value, he will jump one step up with you on the front-end product and service automatically.

Then it will automatically keep moving to middle back end and finally to high-value sales.

The entire process is automated, and customers keep finding a lot of value working with and in return, it will keep moving up the value ladder.

Let me take some examples for Magic Funnel.

1. Trainer or Coaches

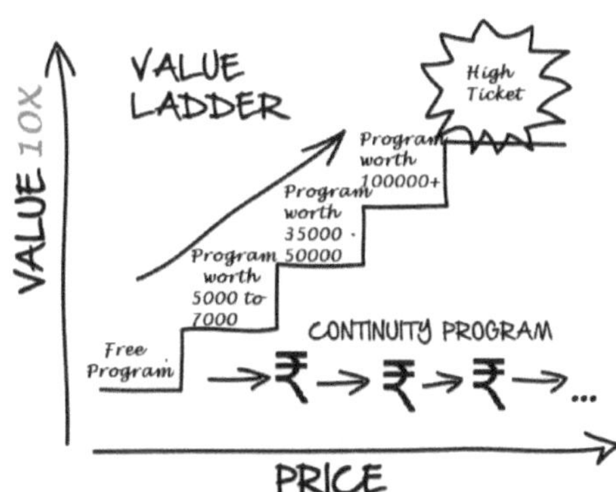

2. Software Product Company

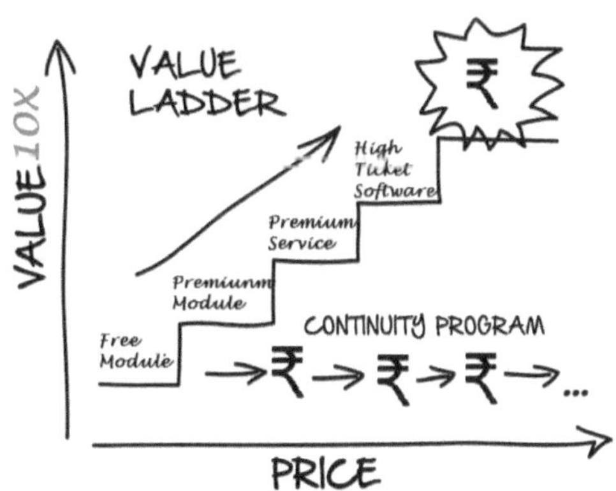

3. **Architecture and Interior Design Company** (Funnel Credit Goes to Sudhir Khollam, He Showed me the working of his company Design India)

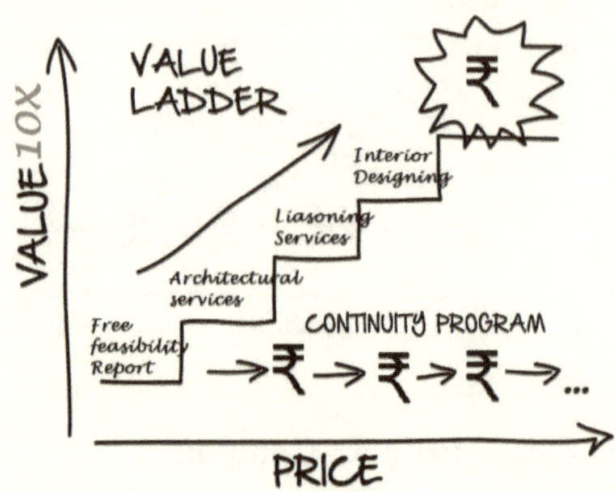

4. **Doctors**

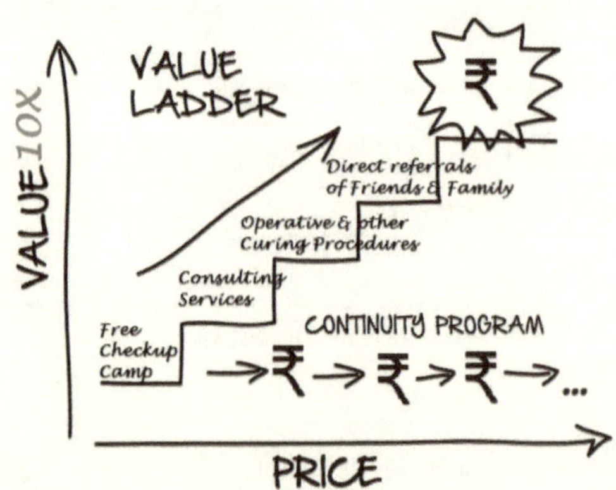

5. Computer IT Hardware Company

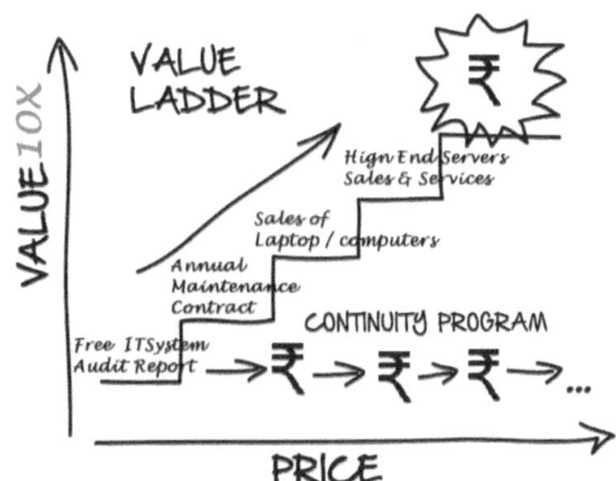

Word of Caution on Funnels

These above examples that I have mentioned above is to illustrate how these funnels should be designed. I guarantee these funnels will not work for you if you just pick these from here and copy-paste in your business. It must be customized as per your company's strengths and core differentiators.

Please work with some experts to design these funnels for your business as yourself trying and implementing in your business may fail you. This will disconnect you from beautiful magic these funnels that can bring lot of success to your business.

Ten core principles to follow to make these funnels work in the long term.

1. Your intent, transparency and desire to help your customer.

2. Healthy marketing plan to continue bringing the lead to bait, even if that is free.

3. Continuous improvement and enhancement of these funnels

4. Bait has a lot of headaches and investment requirements. Earning money is on the backend that is top of the ladder, and soon this customer will climb up the ladder from bait to backend.

5. Brand building exercises

6. High customer service

7. Always create 10X value at every stage

8. Your process should automatically move clients up in the ladder

9. Your sales team should be trained on these funnels

10. Have a mentor to help you set-up and monitor these funnels

Once these funnels start working from bait to high-value sale, you just need to increase investment in marketing and results will improve multifold in your high-value sales.

Some strategies for marketing bait so that you have continuous flow of customers in the funnel:

- Facebook / Instagram Marketing
- WhatsApp marketing

- Google Keyword Marketing
- Linked-In Marketing
- YouTube marketing
- Value-Based Email Marketing (Newsletters)
- Sales Cold Calling
- Authoring Book on your business line
- Website Chat engines

If I start writing on the above marketing strategies, it will be another book. SO learn for a good mentor and implement.

You need to continue INVESTING in marketing for this funnel to work. Fewer people buying your bait will result in fewer people buying your high-ticket products and services.

Once you understand and these funnels start working in your business, it will be a magical growth you have never experienced or expected. That is my commitment to you.

Keep Learning, Keep Growing and
Keep Helping Others to Grow

About Book

Intentionally or unintentionally everyone sells every minute. Some have decided to learn this art and live a successful life. Many have ignored it saying, I have nothing to do with sales as I am not working in the sales department.

Sales is the highest form of Spirituality. Sales is not a profession; instead it is Art of Living a happy and prosperous life. There are many common qualities between extraordinarily successful & effective people and Salesperson.

Do you want to be highly successful in your life?

Do you want to build deep connections with your love without begging for it?

If your answer is yes, then you have the right book in hand. This book will give a new perspective to your life.

Wooing the girl and wooing the customer is same, the only difference is that you only woo one woman at a time and woo many customers together.

Welcome to the world of winners.

DATE YOUR CLIENTS -
WIN HIGH VALUE SALES FROM DATING PRINCIPLES.

About the Author

Kailash C Pinjani an entrepreneur by DNA, and angel investor to many businesses. He follows his passion of growing people with his coaching & training. He has been training thousands of entrepreneurs to create and run successful and profitable businesses. He is an Author Coach; with his mentorship many first-time writers have become successful authors and published their dream book.

Kailash is **#1 Amazon Bestselling Author of the book "Decoding Fitness".**

You can connect to Kailash:

Email: **KailashCPinjani@gmail.com**

Website: **www.kailashpinjani.com**

Instagram: **successcoach.kailash**

About Decoding Fitness

Over the years, Health and fitness concepts are made too difficult to understand. If you are a health enthusiast, trying to gain weight, lose weight, build muscle, or get healthy, you obviously might have come across a lot of confusing and variety of sophisticated advice.

The source of information on what's the "best" way to be healthy and fit can often be daunting. One article will say that eggs, butter, and meat are bad for you. Then another article will say those same things are fantastic for health. Some will say jogging is good for health, and the bodybuilding community will create issues at longer-distance running and will advocate that lifting weights is the best way to get in shape.

You'll get millions of the advice of the best workouts, of when to time your nutrition about eating the kind of food, of how to schedule your workouts, how to measure fitness, what supplements you need to take and...and... and so on.

Sure it's enough to make you want to give up.

But the truth is fitness is very simple that we had disclosed in our book.